Amazon Pinpoint Developer Guide

A catalogue record for this book is available from the Hong Kong Public Libraries.

Published in Hong Kong by Samurai Media Limited.

Email: info@samuraimedia.org

ISBN 9789888408603

Contents

What Is Amazon Pinpoint?

Amazon Pinpoint is an AWS service that you can use to engage with your customers across multiple messaging channels. You can send push notifications, emails, or text messages (SMS), depending on the purpose of your campaign.

This section describes the major features of Amazon Pinpoint.

Define Audience Segments

Reach the right audience for your messages by defining audience segments. A segment designates which users receive the messages that are sent from a campaign. You can define dynamic segments based on data that's reported by your application, such as operating system or mobile device type. You can also import static segments that you define outside of Amazon Pinpoint.

Engage Your Audience with Messaging Campaigns

Engage your audience by creating a messaging campaign. A campaign sends tailored messages on a schedule that you define. You can create campaigns that send mobile push, email, or SMS messages.

To experiment with alternative campaign strategies, set up your campaign as an A/B test, and analyze the results with Amazon Pinpoint analytics.

Send Direct Messages

Keep your customers informed by sending direct mobile push and SMS messages—such as new account activation messages, order confirmations, and password reset notifications—to specific users. You can send direct messages from the Amazon Pinpoint console, or by using the Amazon Pinpoint REST API.

Analyze User Behavior

Gain insights about your audience and the effectiveness of your campaigns by using the analytics that Amazon Pinpoint provides. You can view trends about your users' level of engagement, purchase activity, and demographics. You can monitor your message traffic with metrics for messages sent and opened. Through the Amazon Pinpoint API, your application can report custom data, which Amazon Pinpoint makes available for analysis.

To analyze or store the analytics data outside of Amazon Pinpoint, you can configure Amazon Pinpoint to stream the data to Amazon Kinesis.

Integrate Amazon Pinpoint with Your Applications

Amazon Pinpoint can capture information about the ways your customers interact with your applications. If you're a mobile app developer, you can integrate Amazon Pinpoint into your app code so the app can connect to the service and then report events about app usage. Amazon Pinpoint compiles the app usage events into user engagement analytics that you can use to identify and engage with specific segments of users.

You can use the Amazon Pinpoint API to export application event data, define customer segments, and create and execute multichannel campaigns. You can also use the API to send transactional SMS and mobile push messages directly to specific recipients.

For more information about the Amazon Pinpoint API, see the Amazon Pinpoint API Reference.

AWS SDK Support

One of the easiest ways to interact with the Amazon Pinpoint API is to use an AWS SDK. The following AWS SDKs include support for Amazon Pinpoint API operations:

- AWS Mobile SDK for Android version 2.3.5 or later
- AWS Mobile SDK for iOS version 2.4.14 or later
- AWS SDK for JavaScript version 2.7.10 or later
- AWS SDK for Java version 1.11.63 or later
- AWS SDK for .NET version 3.3.27.0 or later
- AWS SDK for PHP version 3.20.1
- AWS SDK for Python (Boto) version 1.4.2 or later
- AWS SDK for Ruby version 1.0.0.rc2 or later
- AWS SDK for Go version 1.5.13 or later
- AWS SDK for C++ version 1.0.20151208.143 or later

You can also interact with the Amazon Pinpoint API by using version 1.11.24 or later of the AWS Command Line Interface (AWS CLI). The AWS CLI requires Python 2 version 2.6.5 or later, or Python 3 version 3.3 or later. For more information about installing and configuring the AWS CLI, see Installing the AWS Command Line Interface in the *AWS Command Line Interface User Guide*.

Note

The version numbers shown in this section are the first versions of each SDK or CLI that included support for the Amazon Pinpoint API. New resources or operations are occasionally added to the Amazon Pinpoint API. In order to use all of the features of Amazon Pinpoint through the API, ensure that you're using the latest version of the SDK or CLI.

Setting Up Push Notifications for Amazon Pinpoint

Before using Amazon Pinpoint, you must add your app as a project in AWS Mobile Hub. When you add your project, you provide the credentials that authorize Amazon Pinpoint to send messages to your app through the push notification services for iOS and Android:

- For iOS apps, you provide an SSL certificate, which you obtain from the Apple Developer portal. The certificate authorizes Amazon Pinpoint to send messages to your app through Apple Push Notification service (APNs).

- For Android apps, you provide an API Key and a sender ID, which you obtain from the Firebase console or the Google API console. These credentials authorize Amazon Pinpoint to send messages to your app through Firebase Cloud Messaging or its predecessor, Google Cloud Messaging.

After you have the credentials, you can complete the steps in Getting Started: Creating an Mobile App With Amazon Pinpoint Support.

If you already have the credentials, you can skip this section.

- Setting Up iOS Push Notifications
- Setting Up Android Push Notifications

Setting Up iOS Push Notifications

Push notifications for iOS apps are sent using Apple Push Notification service (APNs). Before you can send push notifications to iOS devices, you must create an app ID on the Apple Developer portal, and you must create the required certificates.

This section describes how to use the Apple Developer portal to obtain iOS and APNs credentials. These credentials enable you to create an iOS project in AWS Mobile Hub and launch a sample app that can receive push notifications.

You do not need an existing iOS app to complete the steps in this section. After you create an iOS project in Mobile Hub, you can download and launch a working sample app. Mobile Hub automatically provisions the AWS resources that your app requires.

After completing the steps in this section, you will have the following items in your Apple Developer account:

- An app ID.
- An SSL certificate, which authorizes you to send push notifications to your app through APNs.
- A registration for your test device, such as an iPhone, with your Apple Developer account.
- An iOS distribution certificate, which enables you to install your app on your test device.
- A provisioning profile, which allows your app to run on your test device.

If you already have these items, you can skip this section and complete the steps in Getting Started With iOS Apps.

Before you begin, you must have an account with the Apple Developer Program as an individual or as part of an organization, and you must have agent or admin privileges in that account.

The steps in this tutorial are based on the following versions of Mac OS software:

- OS X El Capitan version 10.11.6
- Xcode version 8.1
- Step 1: Create an App ID
- Step 2: Create an APNs SSL Certificate
- Step 3: Register a Test Device
- Step 4: Create an iOS Distribution Certificate
- Step 5: Create a Provisioning Profile

Step 1: Create an App ID

Create an app ID to identify your app in the Apple Developer portal. You need this ID when you create an SSL certificate for sending push notifications, when you create an iOS distribution certificate, and when you create a provisioning profile.

If you already have an ID assigned to your app, you can skip this step. You can use an existing app ID provided it doesn't contain a wildcard character ("*").

To assign an App ID to your app

1. Sign in to your Apple Developer account at https://developer.apple.com/membercenter/index.action.

2. Choose **Certificates, Identifiers & Profiles**.

Certificates, Identifiers & Profiles

Manage the certificates, identifiers, profiles, and devices you need to develop and distribute apps.

3. In the **Identifiers** section, choose **App IDs**.

ID **Identifiers**

App IDs

Pass Type IDs

Website Push IDs

iCloud Containers

App Groups

4. In the **iOS App IDs** pane, choose the **Add** button (+).

5. In the **Registering an App ID** pane, for **Name**, type a custom name for your app ID that makes it easy to recognize later.

 Registering an App ID

The App ID string contains two parts separated by a period (.)—an App ID Prefix that is defined as your Team ID by default and an App ID Suffix that is defined as a Bundle ID search string. Each part of an App ID has different and important uses for your app. Learn More

App ID Description

Name: exampleApp

You cannot use special characters such as @, &, ', ', "

App ID Prefix

Value: ▓▓▓ ▓▓▓▓ (Team ID)

6. Choose the default selection for an App ID Prefix.

7. For **App ID Suffix**, select **Explicit App ID**, and type a bundle ID for your app. If you already have an app, use the bundle ID assigned to it. You can find this ID in the app project in Xcode on your Mac. Otherwise, take note of the bundle ID because you will assign it to your app in Xcode later.

App ID Suffix

• **Explicit App ID**

If you plan to incorporate app services such as Game Center, In-App Purchase, Data Protection, and iCloud, or want a provisioning profile unique to a single app, you must register an explicit App ID for your app.

To create an explicit App ID, enter a unique string in the Bundle ID field. This string should match the Bundle ID of your app.

Bundle ID: com.exampleCorp.exampleApp

We recommend using a reverse-domain name style string (i.e., com.domainname.appname). It cannot contain an asterisk (*).

Wildcard App ID

8. Under **App Services** select **Push Notifications**.

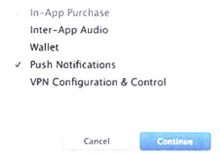

9. Choose **Continue**. In the **Confirm your App ID** pane, check that all values were entered correctly. The identifier should match your app ID and bundle ID.

10. Choose **Register** to register the new app ID.

Step 2: Create an APNs SSL Certificate

Create an APNs SSL certificate so that you can deliver push notifications to your app through APNs. You will create and download the certificate from your Apple Developer account. Then, you will install the certificate in Keychain Access and export it as a .p12 file.

If you already have an SSL certificate for your app, you can skip this step.

To create an SSL certificate for push notifications

1. Sign in to your Apple Developer account at https://developer.apple.com/membercenter/index.action.

2. Choose **Certificates, Identifiers & Profiles**.

Certificates, Identifiers & Profiles

Manage the certificates, identifiers, profiles, and devices you need to develop and distribute apps.

3. From the **Identifiers** section, choose **App IDs**.

ID Identifiers

- App IDs
- Pass Type IDs
- Website Push IDs
- iCloud Containers
- App Groups

4. From the list of iOS app IDs, select the app ID that you created in Step 1: Create an App ID.

5. Choose **Edit**.

6. Under **Push Notifications**, in the **Production SSL Certificate** section, choose **Create Certificate....**

7. In the **About Creating a Certificate Signing Request (CSR)** pane, follow the instructions for creating a Certificate Signing Request (CSR) file. You use the Keychain Access application on your Mac to create the request and save it on your local disk. When you are done, choose **Continue**.

8. In the **Generate your certificate** pane, choose **Choose File...**, and then select the CSR file you created.

Generate your certificate.

When your CSR file is created, a public and private key pair is automatically generated. Your private key is stored on your computer. On a Mac, it is stored in the login Keychain by default and can be viewed in the Keychain Access app under the "Keys" category. Your requested certificate is the public half of your key pair.

Upload CSR file.

Select .certSigningRequest file saved on your Mac.

Choose File...

9. Choose **Continue**.

10. When the certificate is ready, choose **Download** to save the certificate to your computer.

Download, Install and Backup

Download your certificate to your Mac, then double click the .cer file to install in Keychain Access. Make sure to save a backup copy of your private and public keys somewhere secure.

Name:	Apple Development iOS Push Services: **com.exampleCorp.exampleApp**
Type:	APNs Development iOS
Identifier ID:	
Expires:	Dec 06, 2016

Download

Documentation

For more information on using and managing your certificates read:

11. Double-click the downloaded certificate to install it to the Keychain on your Mac.

12. On your Mac, start the Keychain Access application.

13. In **My Certificates**, find the certificate you just added. The certificate is named "Apple Push Services:*com.my.app.id*", where com.my.app.id is the app ID for which the certificate was created.

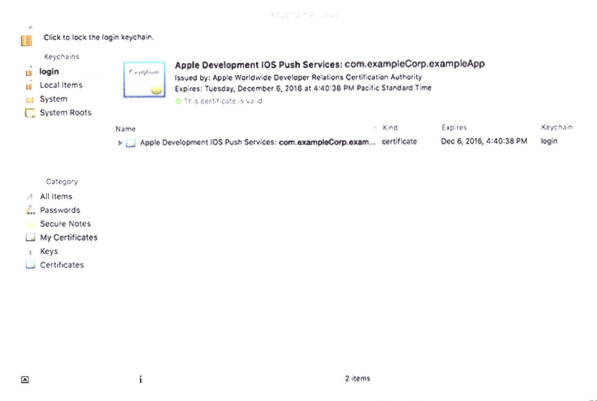

14. Context-select the push certificate and then select **Export...** from the context menu to export a file containing the certificate.

15. Type a name for the certificate that is easy to recognize and save it to your computer. Do not provide an export password when prompted. You need to upload this certificate when creating your app in AWS Mobile Hub.

Step 3: Register a Test Device

Register a test device with your Apple Developer account so that you can test your app on that device. Later, you associate this test device with your provisioning profile, which allows your app to launch on your device.

If you already have a registered device, you can skip this step.

To add a device

1. Sign in to your Apple Developer account at https://developer.apple.com/membercenter/index.action.

2. Choose **Certificates, Identifiers & Profiles**.

Certificates, Identifiers & Profiles

Manage the certificates, identifiers, profiles, and devices you need to develop and distribute apps.

3. In the **Devices** section, choose the type of device that you want to add, such **iPhone**.

4. Choose the **Add** button (+).

5. In the **Register Device** section, for **Name**, type a name that is easy to recognize later.

6. For **UDID**, type the unique device ID. For an iPhone, you can find the UDID by completing the following steps:

   1. Connect your iPhone to your Mac with a USB cable.

   2. Open the iTunes app.

   3. In the top left corner of the iTunes window, a button with an iPhone icon is shown. Choose this button. iTunes displays the summary page for your iPhone.

   4. In the top box, the summary page provides your iPhone's **Capacity**, **Phone Number**, and **Serial Number**. Click **Serial Number**, and the value changes to **UDID**.

   5. Context-select your UDID, and choose **Copy**.

   6. Paste your UDID into the **UDID** field in the Apple Developer website.

7. Choose **Continue**.

8. On the **Review and register** pane, verify the details for your device, and choose **Register**. Your device name and identifier are added to the list of devices.

Step 4: Create an iOS Distribution Certificate

An iOS distribution certificate enables you to install your app on a test device and deliver push notifications to that device. You specify your iOS distribution certificate later when you create a provisioning profile for your app.

If you already have an iOS distribution certificate, you can skip this step.

To create an iOS distribution certificate

1. On the **Certificates, Identifiers & Profiles** page of your Apple Developer account, in the **Certificates section**, choose **Production**.

2. In the **iOS Certificates (Production)** pane, choose the Add button (+). The **Add iOS Certificate** pane opens.

3. In the **Production** section, select **App Store and Ad Hoc**, and then choose **Continue**.

4. On the **About Creating a Certificate Signing Request (CSR)** page, choose **Continue**.

5. In the **About Creating a Certificate Signing Request (CSR)** pane, follow the instructions for creating a Certificate Signing Request (CSR) file. You use the Keychain Access application on your Mac to create the request and save it on your local disk. When you are done, choose **Continue**.

6. In the **Generate your certificate** pane, choose **Choose File...**, and then select the CSR file you created.

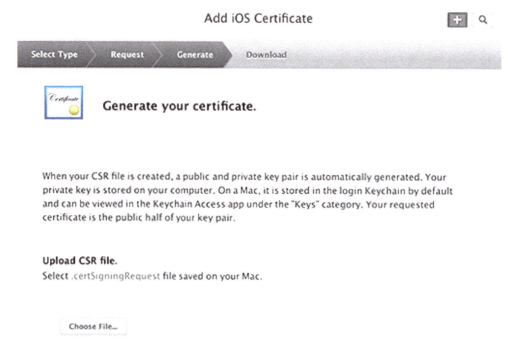

7. Choose **Continue**.

8. When the certificate is ready, choose **Download** to save the certificate to your computer.

9. Double-click the downloaded certificate to install it in Keychain on your Mac.

Step 5: Create a Provisioning Profile

A provisioning profile allows your app to run on your test device. You create and download a provisioning profile from your Apple Developer account and then install the provisioning profile in Xcode.

To create a provisioning profile

1. Sign in to your Apple Developer account at https://developer.apple.com/membercenter/index.action.

2. Select **Certificates, Identifiers & Profiles**.

Certificates, Identifiers & Profiles

Manage the certificates, identifiers, profiles, and devices you need to develop and distribute apps.

3. In the **Provisioning Profiles** section, choose **Distribution**.

4. In the **iOS Provisioning Profiles (Distribution)** pane, choose the add button (+). The **Add iOS Provisioning Profiles (Distribution)** pane is shown.

5. In the **Distribution** section, select **Ad Hoc**, and then choose **Continue**.

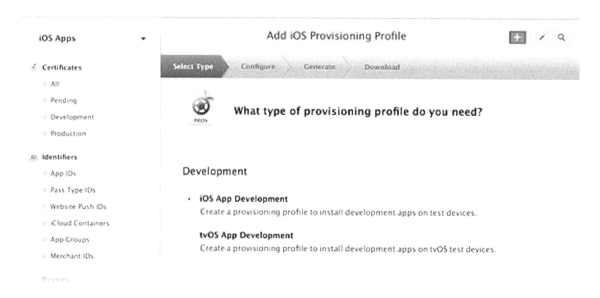

6. For **App ID**, select the app ID you created for your app, and then choose **Continue**.

7. Select your iOS Development certificate and then choose **Continue**.

8. For **Select devices**, select the device that you registered for testing, and choose **Continue**.

9. Type a name for this provisioning profile, such as **ApnsDistributionProfile**, and choose **Continue**.

10. Select **Download** to download the generated provisioning profile.

11. Install the provisioning profile by double-clicking the downloaded file. The Xcode app opens in response.

12. To verify that the provisioning profile is installed, check the list of installed provisioning profiles in Xcode by doing the following:

    1. In the Xcode menu bar, choose **Xcode** and then choose **Preferences**.

    2. In the preferences window, choose **Accounts**.

    3. In the **Accounts** tab, select your Apple ID, and then choose **View Details**.

    4. Check that your provisioning profile is listed in the **Provisioning Profiles** section.

Setting Up Android Push Notifications

This section describes how to obtain the credentials required to send push notifications to Android apps. The platform notification services you can use for push notifications on Android are Firebase Cloud Messaging (FCM) and its predecessor, Google Cloud Messaging (GCM). Your FCM or GCM credentials enable you to create an Android project in AWS Mobile Hub and launch a sample app that can receive push notifications.

You do not need an existing Android app to complete the steps in this section. After you create an Android project in Mobile Hub, you can download and launch a working sample app. Mobile Hub automatically provisions the AWS resources that your app requires.

After completing the steps in this section, you will have an API key and sender ID in the Firebase console or the Google Cloud Platform console. If you already have these credentials, you can skip this section and complete the steps in Getting Started With Android Apps.

- Step 1: Create a Firebase Project
- Step 2: Get Push Messaging Credentials for Android

Step 1: Create a Firebase Project

To send push notifications to Android apps, you must have a project that is enabled with an Android push notification service. The push notification services for Android are Firebase Cloud Messaging (FCM) and its predecessor, Google Cloud Messaging (GCM).

If you are new to push messaging on Android, you must create a Firebase project, as this topic describes. However, if you have an existing Google Cloud Messaging project that has push messaging enabled, you can skip this step and use that project instead.

To create a Firebase project

1. Go to the Firebase console at https://console.firebase.google.com/. If you are not signed in to Google, the link takes you to a sign-in page. After you sign in, you see the Firebase console.

2. Choose **Create New Project**.

3. Type a project name, and then choose **Create Project**.

   Firebase projects support push messaging by default.

Step 2: Get Push Messaging Credentials for Android

To send push notifications to Android apps, you must have credentials from either Firebase Cloud Messaging (FCM) or its predecessor, Google Cloud Messaging (GCM). The credentials are an API key and a sender ID (also called project number). You get these credentials from a project that has push messaging enabled. This project could either be in the Firebase console or the Google Cloud Platform console, depending on where you created it.

This topic describes how to retrieve your credentials from FCM or GCM. Use FCM for new Android apps. Use GCM only if you have a preexisting GCM project that you have not yet updated for FCM support.

To obtain your credentials from FCM

1. Go to the Firebase console at https://console.firebase.google.com/ and open your project.

2. In the left pane, to the right of your project name, choose the gear icon, and then choose **Project Settings**.

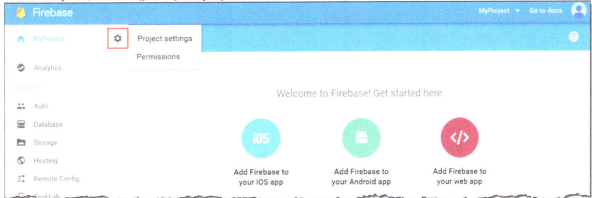

3. In the top menu, choose **Cloud Messaging**.

4. Under **Project credentials**, you find the API key and sender ID. Save these values somewhere you can access later.

To obtain your credentials from GCM

1. Go to the Google API Console at https://console.developers.google.com.

2. In the left pane, choose **Credentials**.

3. If you already have credentials for your app, your server key is shown in the **API keys** section. Save this key somewhere you can access later.

4. If you don't have credentials for your app, the console displays the **Credentials** dialog box. Create a server key by completing the following steps:

1. Choose **Create credentials**.

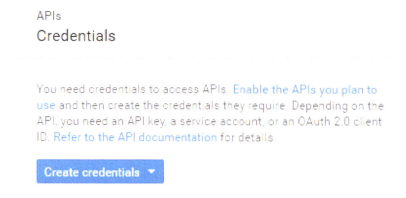

2. Save the API key somewhere you can access later.

5. To retrieve your sender ID (also called project number), go to the Google Cloud Platform console at https://console.cloud.google.com/. Select your project from the **Project** menu. Then, choose the arrow next to the project name.

6. Save the displayed project number somewhere you can access later. **Note** Project number is another name for sender ID.

Getting Started: Creating an Mobile App With Amazon Pinpoint Support

Before you can use Amazon Pinpoint, you must add your app as a project in AWS Mobile Hub and integrate your app with Amazon Pinpoint.

Mobile Hub is an AWS service that helps you create and configure mobile app backend features and integrate them into your app. To add a project and enable Amazon Pinpoint support, you require credentials that authorize Amazon Pinpoint to send push notifications to your app through the push notifications services for Android or iOS. If you need to obtain these credentials, see Setting Up Push Notifications for Amazon Pinpoint.

To integrate your app with Amazon Pinpoint, you download the necessary SDKs from Mobile Hub, and you add these SDKs to your app code.

To test the Amazon Pinpoint features that you enable in Mobile Hub, you download and launch a working sample app. Then, you can use Amazon Pinpoint to create a simple push notification campaign and send a message to the sample app.

If you want to use your own app instead of the Mobile Hub sample app, you can examine the sample app code for guidance on how to include support for push notifications in your own app. The Mobile Hub console also provides steps for integrating the mobile SDKs in your app and enabling Amazon Pinpoint support.

- Getting Started With iOS Apps
- Getting Started With Android Apps
- Testing the Sample App With Amazon Pinpoint

Getting Started With iOS Apps

To add an iOS app to Amazon Pinpoint, create a project in AWS Mobile Hub that has Amazon Pinpoint support.

After you create the project, you can download a functional sample app from Mobile Hub, and run the sample app on a test device that is registered with your Apple Developer account. Then, you can send a push notification to the sample app using Amazon Pinpoint.

- Adding an iOS App to Amazon Pinpoint
- Building the Sample iOS App From AWS Mobile Hub

Adding an iOS App to Amazon Pinpoint

Add an iOS app to Amazon Pinpoint by creating a project in AWS Mobile Hub.

Prerequisite

To complete this task, you need an SSL certificate as a `.p12` file that authorizes Amazon Pinpoint to send push notifications to your app though Apple Push Notification service (APNs). For more information, see Setting Up iOS Push Notifications.

To add an iOS app

1. Sign in to the AWS Management Console and open the Mobile Hub console at https://console.aws.amazon.com/mobilehub.

2. If you have other Mobile Hub projects, choose **Create new mobile project**. If this is your first project, skip this step because you are taken directly to the page for creating a new project.

3. Enter a project name. The name you enter will be the name of your project in the Amazon Pinpoint console.

4. For the region, keep **US East (Virginia)**.

5. Choose **Create project**. Mobile Hub creates the project and shows the **Pick and configure features for your project** page.

6. Choose **Messaging & Analytics**.

7. On the **Messaging & Analytics** page, for **What engagement features do you want to enable?**, choose **Messaging**.

8. For **What Messaging Channels do you want to enable?**, choose **Mobile push**.

9. For **Choose the platforms for which you want to enable push notifications**, choose **iOS**.

10. For **P12 Certificate**, provide the P12 certificate that authorizes Amazon Pinpoint to send push notifications to your app through Apple Push Notification service (APNs). Then, choose **Upload**.

11. Choose **Enable**.

Mobile Hub helps you integrate Amazon Pinpoint with your app in two ways:

1. You can download a working sample app that demonstrates Amazon Pinpoint features. Then, you can build the sample app and send it a push notification with Amazon Pinpoint.

2. You can download a package that includes the required SDKs for your project. Then, you can follow the instructions in the AWS Mobile Hub console to integrate Amazon Pinpoint with your app.

Now that you have created a Mobile Hub project for your app, you can see your app in the Amazon Pinpoint console at https://console.aws.amazon.com/pinpoint/.

Building the Sample iOS App From AWS Mobile Hub

To test the Amazon Pinpoint features that you enabled in AWS Mobile Hub, build the sample iOS app and launch it on a test device. Then, create a simple push notification campaign in Amazon Pinpoint and send a message to the sample app.

Prerequisites
To complete this task, you need:
A Mobile Hub sample iOS app with Amazon Pinpoint support. If you need to create the sample app, see Adding an iOS App to Amazon Pinpoint. A Mac with Xcode installed. The following procedure is based on OS X El Capitan version 10.11.6 and Xcode version 8.1. The following items from the Apple Developer portal:
An app ID. A registration for a test device (such as an iPhone). An iOS distribution certificate installed in Keychain on your Mac. An Ad Hoc distribution provisioning profile installed in Xcode on your Mac. If you need to obtain these items, see Setting Up iOS Push Notifications.

To build the sample app

1. In the AWS Mobile Hub console, on the **Integrate** page for your app, choose **Download a sample app**, and save the sample app to your local drive.

2. Browse to the package you downloaded and open the `MySampleApp.xcodeproj` file to open the sample app in Xcode.

3. Open the target for the sample app project, and choose **General**.

4. In the **Identity** section, for **Display Name**, type a custom display name to make the sample app easy to recognize after you install it on your device, such as **Pnpt Sample**.

5. For **Bundle Identifier**, type the bundle ID associated with the provisioning profile for your app.

6. In the **Signing (Debug)** and **Signing (Release)** sections, for **Provisioning Profile**, select your provisioning profile. Xcode shows only those provisioning profiles that are associated with the bundle ID that you provided.

7. In the **Product** menu, choose **Archive**.

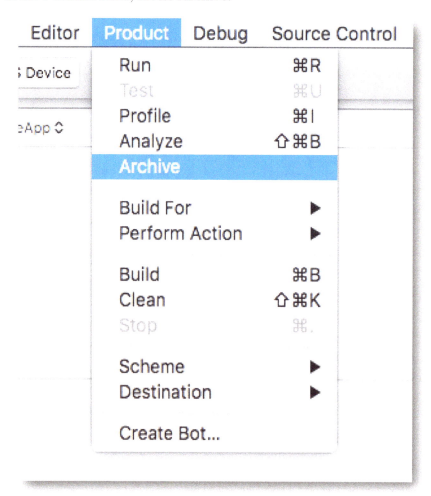

8. In the **Archives** window, choose **Export**.

9. In the **Select a method for export** window, select **Save for Ad Hoc Deployment**, and choose **Next**.

10. When prompted, choose your development team.

11. In the **Device Support** window, select **Export one app for all compatible devices**, and choose **Next**.

12. In the **Summary** window, choose **Next**.

13. Browse to the location on your local drive where you want to save the exported .ipa file, and choose **Export**.

To launch the sample app on your test device

1. Connect your device to your Mac with a USB cable.

2. In the Xcode menu bar, choose **Window**, and then choose **Devices**.

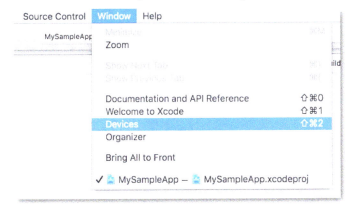

3. In the **Devices** section, select your device.

4. In the **Installed Apps** section, choose the plus icon.

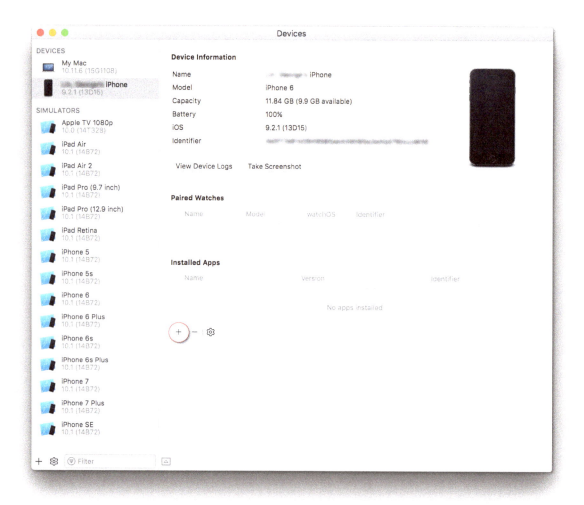

5. Browse to the location of your exported `.ipa` file, select it, and choose **Open**. The sample app is installed, and you can see the app icon on your device.

6. Launch the app on your device. If this your first time launching an app signed with your distribution certificate, you receive an **Untrusted Developer** message, and the app won't launch.

Before you can open your app, you must trust your distribution certificate on your device. Tap **Settings**, **General**, and finally **Device Management**. Then, tap the distribution certificate, tap **Trust**, and when prompted, tap **Trust**.

Launch the app again.

7. When the app requests permission to send you notifications, tap **Allow**.

8. In the sample app, you can tap **User Sign-in** or **User Engagement** to learn more about these features.

My Sample App

User Sign-in
Enable user login with popular 3rd party providers.

User Engagement
Analyze app usage, define segments, create and measure campaign metrics.

Now that you have built the sample iOS app, you can test the app by sending it a push notification from Amazon Pinpoint.

Getting Started With Android Apps

To add an Android app to Amazon Pinpoint, create a project in AWS Mobile Hub that has Amazon Pinpoint support.

After you create the project, you can download a functional sample app from Mobile Hub, and run the sample app in an Android emulator using Android Studio. Then, you can send a push notification to the sample app using Amazon Pinpoint.

- Adding an Android App to Amazon Pinpoint
- Creating an Android Virtual Device
- Building the Sample Android App From AWS Mobile Hub

Adding an Android App to Amazon Pinpoint

Add an Android app to Amazon Pinpoint by creating a project in AWS Mobile Hub.

Prerequisite
To complete this task, you need:
A project that has push messaging enabled with Firebase or Google Cloud Platform. For more information, see Step 1: Create a Firebase Project. A Firebase Cloud Messaging (FCM) or Google Cloud Messaging (GCM) API key and a sender ID (also called project number). For more information, see Step 2: Get Push Messaging Credentials for Android.

To add an Android app

1. Sign in to the AWS Management Console and open the Mobile Hub console at https://console.aws.amazon.com/mobilehub.

2. If you have other Mobile Hub projects, choose **Create new mobile project**. If this is your first project, skip this step because you are taken directly to the page for creating a new project.

3. Enter a project name. The name you enter will be the name of your project in the Amazon Pinpoint console.

4. For the region, keep **US East (Virginia)**.

5. Choose **Create project**. Mobile Hub creates the project and shows the **Pick and configure features for your project** page.

6. Choose **Messaging & Analytics**.

7. On the **Messaging & Analytics** page, for **What engagement features do you want to enable?**, choose **Messaging**.

8. For **What Messaging Channels do you want to enable?**, choose **Mobile push**.

9. For **Choose the platforms for which you want to enable push notifications**, choose **Android**.

10. Enter your **API key** and **Sender ID**, which are available from your project that has push messaging enabled in Firebase or Google Cloud Platform. In Google Cloud Platform, the sender ID is called project number.

11. Choose **Enable**.

Mobile Hub helps you integrate Amazon Pinpoint with your app in two ways:

1. You can download a working sample app that demonstrates Amazon Pinpoint features. Then, you can create a virtual device and build the sample app so that you can send it a push notification with Amazon Pinpoint.

2. You can download a package that includes the required SDKs for your project. Then, you can follow the instructions in the AWS Mobile Hub console to integrate Amazon Pinpoint with your app.

Creating an Android Virtual Device

To send push notifications from Amazon Pinpoint to an Android app, you must install the app on an Android device. For testing purposes, you can use a virtual device. This topic describes how to create a virtual device in Android Studio. If you have a physical Android device and know how to install apps onto it using Android Studio, you can skip this step.

This topic helps you create a virtual device of type Nexus 6 phone with Lollipop API Level 22 x86 Android 5.1, but the AWS Mobile Hub quickstart app is not limited to this device. You can use any device that uses Android OS 4.0.3 (IceCreamSandwich) API Level 15 or higher.

To create a virtual device with Android Studio

1. Open Android Studio.

2. From the **Tools** menu, choose **Android**, and then choose **AVD Manager**.

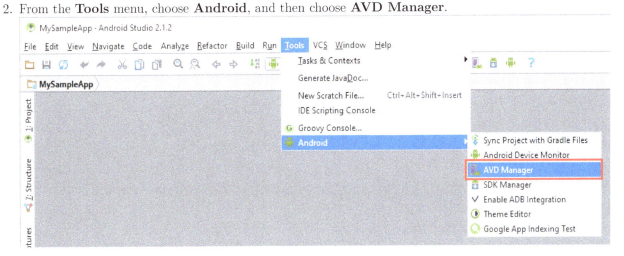

3. On the **Your Virtual Devices** page, choose **Create Virtual Device**.

4. On the **Select Hardware** page, choose **Nexus 6**, and then choose **Next**.

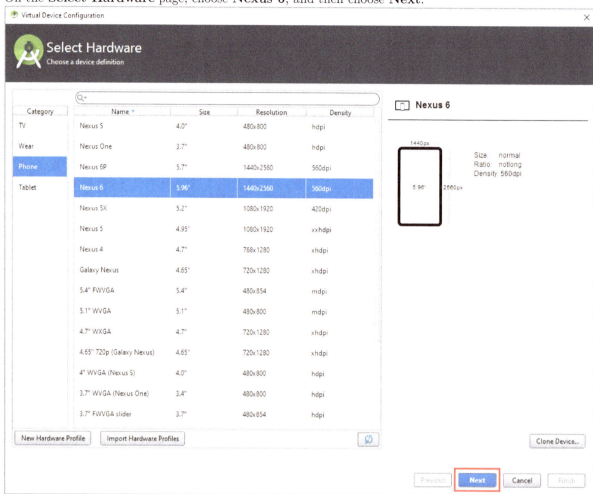

5. On the **System Image** page, choose the system image with **Release name** Lollipop, **API Level** 22, **ABI** x86, and **Target** Android 5.1 (with Google APIs), and then choose **Next**.

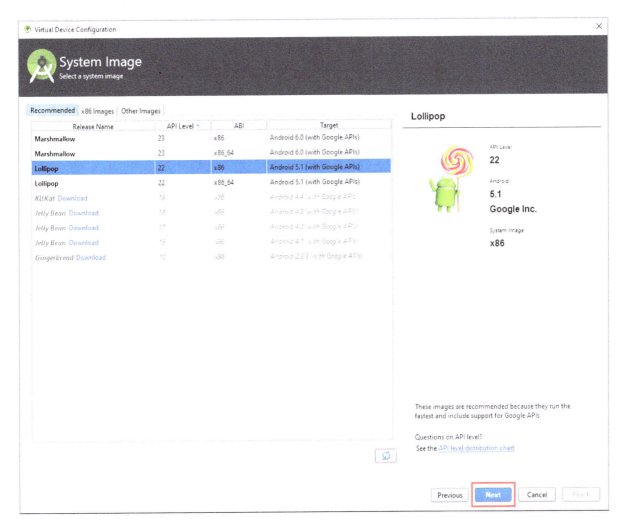

6. On the **Android Virtual Device** page, choose **Finish**.

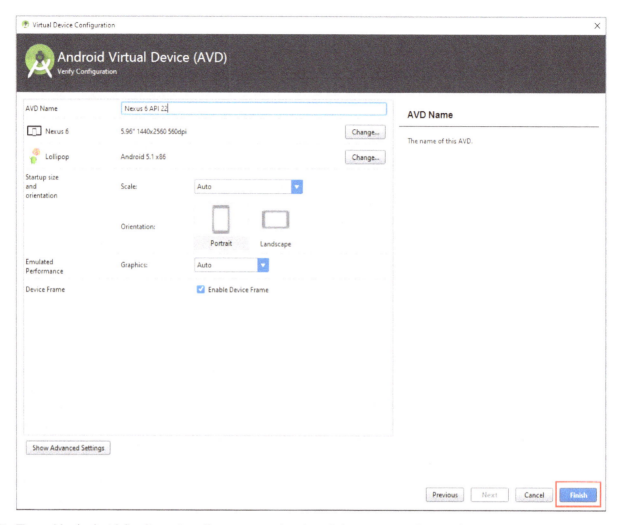

7. To enable Android Studio to install an app on the virtual device, go to the **Tools** menu, choose **Android**, and then choose **Enable ADB Integration**.

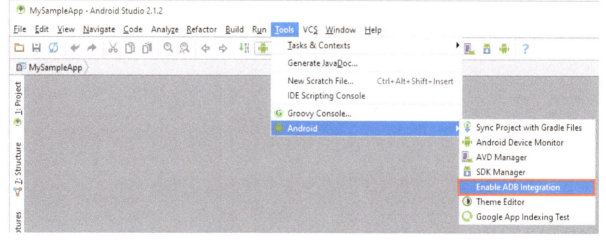

Building the Sample Android App From AWS Mobile Hub

This topic describes how to import and build the AWS Mobile Hub sample app code in Android Studio. We assume that you have generated the quickstart app code using the AWS Mobile Hub console, and downloaded the code in the .zip file to your computer.

Prerequisites
To complete this task, you need:
A Mobile Hub sample Android app with Amazon Pinpoint support. If you need to create the sample app, see Adding an Android App to Amazon Pinpoint. Android Studio with the following SDK support, which you can download from https://developer.android.com/studio/index.html:
Android Studio 1.4 or newer Android SDK 4.4 (KitKat) API Level 19 or newer Android SDK Build-tools 23.0.1 A physical or virtual Android device with Android OS 4.0.3 (IceCreamSandwich) API Level 15 or newer and Google Play Services.

To build the AWS Mobile Hub sample app

1. Unzip the .zip file that you downloaded from AWS Mobile Hub.

2. Open Android Studio and choose **Import project (Eclipse ADT, Gradle, etc.)**.

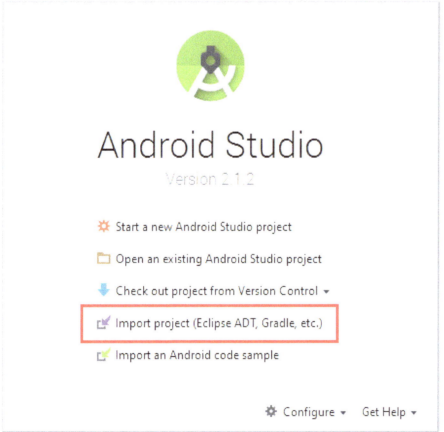

3. Open the folder where you extracted the .zip file contents and choose the **MySampleApp** folder.

   Android Studio imports the project and builds it using Gradle.

4. If a dialog box appears recommending that you update your Gradle Plug-in, choose **Don't remind me again for this project**.

After the build completes, you can install and run the app on a physical or virtual Android device.

To run the app on a virtual Android device

1. In Android Studio, choose the run icon in the toolbar.

2. In the **Select a Deployment Target** window, select your virtual device, and choose **OK**. The Android emulator opens, and the sample app launches in the virtual device. You can choose **User Sign-in** or **User Engagement** to learn more about these features.

3. In the Android emulator, sign in to your Google account so that the sample app can receive push notifications from Amazon Pinpoint:

   1. Open **Settings**.

   2. Choose **Accounts**.

   3. Choose **Add account**, **Google**, and provide your Google email address and password.

Testing the Sample App With Amazon Pinpoint

To verify that your AWS Mobile Hub sample app can receive push notifications from Amazon Pinpoint, use Amazon Pinpoint to create a simple campaign and send a message to the app.

Prerequisite
To complete this task, you need a Mobile Hub sample app with Amazon Pinpoint support. To receive push notifications, you must build the sample app and run it. For more information, see Getting Started With iOS Apps or Getting Started With Android Apps.

To send a push notification to the sample app

1. Sign in to the AWS Management Console and open the Amazon Pinpoint console at https://console.aws.amazon.com/pinpoint/.

2. On the **Projects** page, choose the app that you created in AWS Mobile Hub.

3. Unless you have already created a campaign for your app, the console shows the **Campaigns** page. Choose **New campaign** to create a campaign.

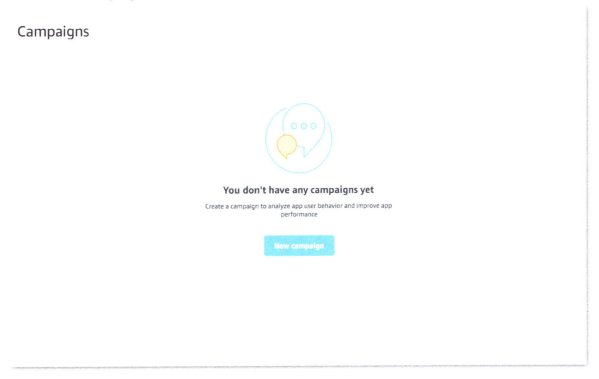

4. The **Create a campaign** page displays at the **Details** step.

5. For **Name your campaign**, type a name to make the campaign easy to recognize later.

6. For **Choose the type of your campaign**, choose **Standard campaign**.

7. Choose **Next step**, and the console displays the **Segments** step.

8. Keep the default options for the segment, which include users who have used your app in the last 30 days. The **Segment estimate** count indicates how many user endpoints your campaign will deliver messages to. Because you built the sample app for iOS or Android and ran that app, you will see a segment estimate of 1 if your app successfully registered as an endpoint with Amazon Pinpoint.

9. Choose **Next step**. The console displays the **Message** step.

10. Keep **Standard notification** selected, and type a title and message for your test push notification.

11. For **Action**, keep **Open app**.

12. Choose **Next step**. The console displays the **Schedule** step.

13. Choose **Immediate**, and then choose **Next step**. The console displays the **Review and launch** step.

14. Choose **Launch campaign**. Amazon Pinpoint delivers your test push notification to the sample app on your test device.

Integrating Amazon Pinpoint with a Mobile App

To take advantage of Amazon Pinpoint, your mobile app must incorporate code that records and submits analytics data to the Amazon Pinpoint service. This section describes concepts you need to know to incorporate Amazon Pinpoint into a mobile app using the AWS Mobile SDK APIs.

To integrate the code that makes data collection possible, use the APIs provided by the AWS Mobile SDK for iOS and AWS Mobile SDK for Android. When working on platforms other than those supported by the AWS Mobile SDK, use the REST API to access Amazon Pinpoint.

- Integrating Amazon Pinpoint With iOS Apps
- Integrating Amazon Pinpoint with Android Apps

Integrating Amazon Pinpoint With iOS Apps

To use Amazon Pinpoint with an iOS app, you must integrate code that connects your app to Amazon Pinpoint. This enables the app to send event data used by the service to track user activity and gather engagement metrics.

- Setting Up the AWS Mobile SDK for iOS
- Initializing the Amazon Pinpoint Client
- Registering Endpoints
- Reporting Events
- Handling Push Notifications

Setting Up the AWS Mobile SDK for iOS

Before modifying your app to use Amazon Pinpoint, set up the AWS Mobile SDK for iOS.

To set up the AWS Mobile SDK for iOS

1. Open your app project in Xcode.

2. Context-click in your project tree view, and select **Add files to ""...** from the context menu.

3. Locate the `AWSCore.framework` and `AWSPinpoint.framework` files from the downloaded .zip file. Select the files, and choose **Add**.

4. Open a target for your project, select **Build Phases**, expand **Link Binary With Libraries**. Then, click the + button, and add:

   - libsqlite3

   - libz

   - SystemConfiguration.framework

5. Open the target for your project, choose **General** and expand the **Embedded Binaries** section. Then, choose the plus icon (+).

6. In the window that opens, select the AWSCore and AWSPinpoint frameworks.

7. Choose **Capabilities**. Enable push notification and remote notifications in background modes.

8. Edit your `Info.plist` file to include your AWS information:

```
1  <?xml version="1.0" encoding="UTF-8"?>
2  <!DOCTYPE plist PUBLIC "-//Apple//DTD PLIST 1.0//EN" "http://www.apple.com/DTDs/
      PropertyList-1.0.dtd">
3  <plist version="1.0">
4  <dict>
5   <key>AWS</key>
6   <dict>
7      <key>CredentialsProvider</key>
8      <dict>
9         <key>CognitoIdentity</key>
10        <dict>
11           <key>Default</key>
12           <dict>
13              <key>PoolId</key>
14              <string>IDENTITY_POOL_ID</string>
15              <key>Region</key>
16              <string>us-east-1</string>
17           </dict>
18        </dict>
19     </dict>
20     <key>PinpointAnalytics</key>
21     <dict>
22        <key>Default</key>
23        <dict>
24           <key>AppId</key>
25           <string>APP_ID</string>
26           <key>Region</key>
27           <string>us-east-1</string>
28        </dict>
```

```
29      </dict>
30      <key>PinpointTargeting</key>
31      <dict>
32          <key>Default</key>
33          <dict>
34              <key>Region</key>
35              <string>us-east-1</string>
36          </dict>
37      </dict>
38  </dict>
39 </dict>
```

9. If, when a user taps a push notification sent to your app, you want your app to open a URL, add the following:

```
1 <key>LSApplicationQueriesSchemes</key>
2 <array>
3  <string>http</string>
4  <string>https</string>
5 </array>
```

Initializing the Amazon Pinpoint Client

After you have included AWS Mobile SDK for Android support in your app, which enables the app to call AWS services, modify the app code to initialize the Amazon Pinpoint client.

Add the following import to your main activity:

```
1  import com.amazonaws.mobileconnectors.pinpoint.*;
```

Depending on how your app authenticates calls, you may also need to add the following import:

```
1  import com.amazonaws.regions.Regions;
```

Important

For simplicity, the code in these examples initializes the Amazon Pinpoint client in the onCreate method. This approach can take several seconds to execute. In production code, this initialization is best done in a background thread. For more information about how to do this, see the Google Developer website.

To initialize the Amazon Pinpoint client using the default initializer

- Initialize the Amazon Pinpoint client as follows:

```
1  CognitoCachingCredentialsProvider cognitoCachingCredentialsProvider = new
       CognitoCachingCredentialsProvider(context,"IDENTITY_POOL_ID",Regions.US_EAST_1);
2
3  PinpointConfiguration config = new PinpointConfiguration(context, "APP_ID", Regions.US_EAST_1,
       cognitoCachingCredentialsProvider);
4
5  this.pinpointManager = new PinpointManager(config);
```

Registering Endpoints

When a user starts an app session (the app comes to the foreground), the AWS Mobile SDK for Android automatically registers (or updates) an *endpoint* with Amazon Pinpoint. In this case, an endpoint represents a unique user's mobile device. The endpoint includes attributes that describe the device, and can also include other attributes that you define.

After your app registers endpoints, you can segment your audience based on endpoint attributes, and you can engage these segments with tailored messaging campaigns. You can also use the **Analytics** page in the Amazon Pinpoint console to view charts about endpoint registration and activity, such as **New endpoints** and **Daily active endpoints**.

You can assign a single user ID to multiple endpoints. In the context of mobile applications, a user ID represents a single user, while the endpoints associated with the user ID represent the devices that the user uses to interact with your app. Endpoints can also represent other methods of communicating with customers, such as email addresses or mobile phone numbers. For more information, see Adding Endpoints. After you assign user IDs to your endpoints, you can view charts about user activity in the console, such as **Daily active users** and **Monthly active users**.

Adding Custom Endpoint Attributes

You can add custom attributes to the device profile as shown in the following example, which adds a `favoriteTeams` custom attribute.

In the following example, the `AWSMobileClient` class is provided in the AWS Mobile Hub sample code to reference the Amazon Pinpoint object.

```
1 AWSMobileClient.defaultMobileClient()
2     .getPinpointManager().getTargetingClient().addAttribute("favoriteTeams", Arrays.asList(new
        String[]{"Lakers", "Clippers"}));
3 AWSMobileClient.defaultMobileClient()
4     .getPinpointManager().getTargetingClient().updateEndpointProfile();
```

Assigning User IDs to Endpoints

Assign user IDs to endpoints by doing either of the following:

- Manage user sign-up and sign-in with Amazon Cognito user pools.
- Use the `PinpointManager` class to assign user IDs to endpoints.

Amazon Cognito user pools provide user directories that make it easier to add sign-up and sign-in to your app. When the Mobile SDK for Android registers an endpoint with Amazon Pinpoint, Amazon Cognito automatically assigns a user ID from the user pool. For more information, see Using Amazon Pinpoint Analytics with Amazon Cognito User Pools in the *Amazon Cognito Developer Guide*.

If you don't want to use Amazon Cognito user pools, you can use the `TargetingClient` of the `PinpointManager` class to assign user IDs to endpoints, as shown in the following example.

```
1 EndpointProfile profile = this.pinpointManager.getTargetingClient().currentEndpoint();
2 profile.getUser().setUserId("UserIdValue");
3 this.pinpointManager.getTargetingClient().updateEndpointProfile(profile);
```

Reporting Events

You can use the AWS Mobile SDK for Android to report app usage data, or *events*, to Amazon Pinpoint. Report events to capture information such as app session times, users' purchasing behavior, sign-in attempts, or any custom event type that serves your needs.

After your app reports events, view app analytics in the Amazon Pinpoint console. The charts on the **Analytics** page provide metrics for many aspects of user behavior. For more information, see Chart Reference for Amazon Pinpoint Analytics in the *Amazon Pinpoint User Guide*.

To analyze and store your event data outside of Amazon Pinpoint, you can configure Amazon Pinpoint to stream the data to Amazon Kinesis. For more information, see Streaming Amazon Pinpoint Events to Kinesis.

Recording Monetization Events

To track the revenue that is generated by your app and the number of items purchased by users, update your app code to report monetization events.

After your app reports monetization events, view revenue analytics in the Amazon Pinpoint console. On the **Analytics** page, the **Revenue** tab provides charts for **Revenue**, **Paying users**, **Units sold**, and more.

The following example uses the `AnalyticsClient` of the `PinpointManager` class to record and submit a monetization event.

```
1 final AnalyticsEvent event = GooglePlayMonetizationEventBuilder.create(AWSMobileClient.
     defaultMobileClient()
2        .getPinpointManager().getAnalyticsClient())
3   .withCurrency("USD")
4   .withItemPrice(1.00)
5   .withProductId("PRODUCT_ID")
6   .withQuantity(1.0)
7   .withTransactionId("TRANSACTION_ID").build();
8 AWSMobileClient.defaultMobileClient()
9        .getPinpointManager().getAnalyticsClient().recordEvent(event);
10 AWSMobileClient.defaultMobileClient()
11        .getPinpointManager().getAnalyticsClient().submitEvents();
```

Reporting Authentication Events

To learn how frequently users authenticate with your app, update your app code so that Amazon Pinpoint receives the following standard event types for authentication:

- `_userauth.sign_in`
- `_userauth.sign_up`
- `_userauth.auth_fail`

After Amazon Pinpoint receives these event types, use the **Analytics** page in the Amazon Pinpoint console to view charts for **Sign-ins**, **Sign-ups**, and **Authentication failures**.

You can report authentication events by doing either of the following:

- Managing user sign-up and sign-in with Amazon Cognito user pools.
- Submitting events with the `PinpointManager` class.

Amazon Cognito user pools provide user directories that make it easier to add sign-up and sign-in to your app. As users authenticate with your app, Amazon Cognito reports authentication events to Amazon Pinpoint. For more information, see Using Amazon Pinpoint Analytics with Amazon Cognito User Pools in the *Amazon Cognito Developer Guide*.

If you don't want to use Amazon Cognito user pools, you can use the `AnalyticsClient` of the `PinpointManager` class to record and submit authentication events, as shown in the following example. The event type is set to `_userauth.sign_in`, but you can substitute any authentication event type.

```
1  final AnalyticsEvent event =  AWSMobileClient.defaultMobileClient()
2          .getPinpointManager().getAnalyticsClient().createEvent("_userauth.sign_in")
3  AWSMobileClient.defaultMobileClient()
4          .getPinpointManager().getAnalyticsClient().recordEvent(event);
5  AWSMobileClient.defaultMobileClient()
6          .getPinpointManager().getAnalyticsClient().submitEvents();
```

Reporting Custom Events

A custom event must have an event type, and you can add custom attributes and metrics to that event.

In the following example, the `AWSMobileClient` class is provided in the AWS Mobile Hub sample code to reference the Amazon Pinpoint object.

```
1  final AnalyticsEvent event =  AWSMobileClient.defaultMobileClient()
2          .getPinpointManager().getAnalyticsClient().createEvent("MyCustomEvent")
3      // A music app use case might include attributes such as:
4      // .withAttribute("Playlist", "Amazing Songs 2016")
5      // .withAttribute("Artist", "Various")
6      // .withMetric("Song playtime", playTime);
7      .withAttribute("MyAttribute1", "MyAttributeValue1")
8      .withAttribute("MyAttribute2", "MyAttributeValue2")
9      .withMetric("MyMetric1", Math.random());
10
11 AWSMobileClient.defaultMobileClient()
12         .getPinpointManager().getAnalyticsClient().recordEvent(event);
13 AWSMobileClient.defaultMobileClient()
14         .getPinpointManager().getAnalyticsClient().submitEvents();
```

Handling Push Notifications

The following topics describe how to modify your Android app so that it receives push notifications sent by Amazon Pinpoint. You can send notifications to Android apps with multiple push notification services, each of which is supported with an Amazon Pinpoint channel. Each push notification service has unique requirements for updating your app code.

- Handling Push Notifications from Firebase Cloud Messaging or Google Cloud Messaging
- Handling Push Notifications from Amazon Device Messaging
- Handling Push Notifications from Baidu Cloud Push
- Setting up Deep Linking

Handling Push Notifications from Apple Push Notification Service

Modify your app code to handle push notifications from Apple Push Notification service (APNs).

Registering for Push Notifications

Prompt the user to accept receiving push notifications during app launch or when the app requests receipt of push notifications. After the user grants permission, the app should re-register when launching the app because the device token can change.

[Objective-C]

```objc
1 UIUserNotificationType userNotificationTypes =
2     (UIUserNotificationTypeAlert | UIUserNotificationTypeBadge |
3         UIUserNotificationTypeSound);
4 UIUserNotificationSettings *notificationSettings =
5     [UIUserNotificationSettings settingsForTypes:userNotificationTypes
6         categories:nil];
7
8 [[UIApplication sharedApplication]
9     registerUserNotificationSettings:notificationSettings];
```

[Swift]

```swift
1 let settings = UIUserNotificationSettings(
2     forTypes: [.Sound, .Alert, .Badge], categories: nil)
3
4 UIApplication.sharedApplication().registerUserNotificationSettings(settings)
5 UIApplication.shared().registerForRemoteNotifications()
```

If you are using iOS 10 or greater with the `UserNotification` framework, add the following:

[Objective-C]

```objc
1 [UNUserNotificationCenter currentNotificationCenter]
2 requestAuthorizationWithOptions:(UNAuthorizationOptionAlert +
3     UNAuthorizationOptionSound)
4 completionHandler:^(BOOL granted, NSError * _Nullable error) {
5   // Enable or disable features based on authorization.
6 }];
7 [[UIApplication sharedApplication] registerForRemoteNotifications];
```

[Swift]

```
1 UNUserNotificationCenter.current().requestAuthorization(options:[.badge, .alert, .sound]) {
2   (granted, error) in
3   // Enable or disable features based on authorization.
4 }
5 UIApplication.shared().registerForRemoteNotifications()
```

Handle Notification Callbacks

To enable Amazon Pinpoint to report the notifications that are opened for a campaign, you must intercept some notification callbacks.

In the application:didRegisterForRemoteNotificationsWithDeviceToken: method in the ApplicationDelegate for your app, call the interceptor:

[Objective-C]

```
1 -(void)application:(UIApplication * )application
2     didRegisterForRemoteNotificationsWithDeviceToken:(NSData *)deviceToken {
3   [_pinpoint.notificationManager
4       interceptDidRegisterForRemoteNotificationsWithDeviceToken:deviceToken];
```

[Swift]

```
1 func application(application: UIApplication,
2     didRegisterForRemoteNotificationsWithDeviceToken deviceToken: NSData) {
3   pinpoint!.notificationManager
4       .interceptDidRegisterForRemoteNotificationsWithDeviceToken(deviceToken)
```

In the application:didReceiveNotification:fetchCompletionHandler: method in the ApplicationDelegate for your app, call the interceptor:

[Objective-C]

```
1 -(void)application:(UIApplication * )application
2     didReceiveRemoteNotification:(nonnull NSDictionary *)userInfo
3     fetchCompletionHandler:(nonnull void (^)(UIBackgroundFetchResult))
4     completionHandler {
5   [_pinpoint.notificationManager interceptDidReceiveRemoteNotification:
6       userInfofetchCompletionHandler:completionHandler];
7   completionHandler(UIBackgroundFetchResultNewData);
```

[**Swift**]

```
1  func application(application: UIApplication,
2      didReceiveRemoteNotification userInfo: [NSObject : AnyObject],
3      fetchCompletionHandler completionHandler: (UIBackgroundFetchResult) -> Void) {
4    pinpoint!.notificationManager.interceptDidReceiveRemoteNotification(
5        userInfo, fetchCompletionHandler: completionHandler)
```

If you are using iOS 10 or greater with the UserNotification framework, add the following:

[**Objective-C**]

```
1  -(void)userNotificationCenter:(UNUserNotificationCenter * ) center
2      didReceiveNotificationResponse: (UNNotificationResponse * ) response
3      withCompletionHandler: (void( ^ )(void)) completionHandler {
4    [[[AWSMobileClient sharedInstance] pinpoint].notificationManager
5        interceptDidReceiveRemoteNotification:
6        response.notification.request.content.userInfo
7        fetchCompletionHandler: ^ (UIBackgroundFetchResult result) {}
8    ];
```

[**Swift**]

```
1  @available(iOS 10.0, *)
2  func userNotificationCenter(center: UNUserNotificationCenter,
3      didReceiveNotificationResponse response: UNNotificationResponse,
4      withCompletionHandler completionHandler: () -> Void) {
5    pinpoint!.notificationManager.interceptDidReceiveRemoteNotification(
6        response.notification.request.content.userInfo) {
7          (UIBackgroundFetchResult) in
8        }
```

Setting Up Deep Linking

Amazon Pinpoint campaigns can take one of three actions when a user taps a notification. One of those possible actions is a deep link, which opens the app to a specified activity.

Registering a Custom URL Scheme

To specify a destination activity for deep links, the app must have set up deep linking. This setup requires registering a custom URL scheme the deep links will use. To register a custom URL identifier, go to your Xcode project's target **Info** tab and expand the **URL Types** section.

To open the app via a `pinpoint://` URL scheme you need to assign a unique identifier to the scheme. Apple recommends reverse DNS notation to avoid name collisions on the platform. The following example uses `com.exampleCorp.exampleApp`:

To register a custom URL scheme in Xcode:

1. In Xcode, select the **Info** tab.

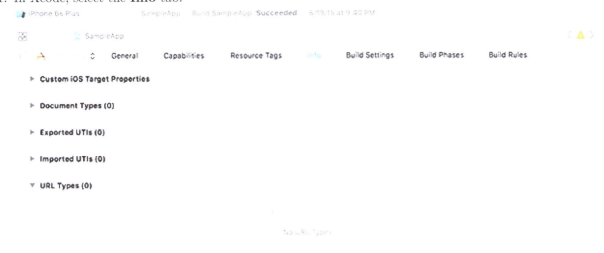

2. In the **URL Types** section, select + to add a URL type.

3. Enter the reverse DNS notation identifier for this URL type in **Identifier**.

4. Enter the URL you want to use for your app in **URL Schemes**.

5. Save the project.

After this custom URL scheme is registered, test it in the iOS simulator. Open Safari and navigate to your custom URL; in this example, `pinpoint://`. Your app launches and opens to its home screen.

Listening for Custom URLs

To direct the app to a specific view, implement a callback in your `AppDelegate` that is called when your app launches from a deep link. The scheme launches the app, using the host and path to go to a separate screen within the app. The following example from the sample application shows how to implement a deep link in your application. This link takes the user to page1 if it receives a `pinpoint://deeplink/page1` link.

Objective-C

```objectivec
-(BOOL) application: (UIApplication * ) application openURL: (NSURL * ) url sourceApplication: (
    NSString * ) sourceApplication annotation: (id) annotation {
  NSLog(@ "%s", __func__);
  if ([[url host] isEqualToString: @ "deeplink"]) {
    if ([[url path] isEqualToString: @ "/page1"]) {
      dispatch_after(dispatch_time(DISPATCH_TIME_NOW, (int64_t)(1 * NSEC_PER_SEC)),
          dispatch_get_main_queue(), ^ {
        [((UINavigationController * ) self.window.rootViewController)
            popToRootViewControllerAnimated: NO];
        [
          [((UINavigationController * ) self.window.rootViewController).viewControllers
              firstObject] performSegueWithIdentifier: @ "PAGE1_SEGUE"
          sender: self.window.rootViewController
        ];
      });
    }
    else if ([[url path] isEqualToString: @ "/page2"]) {
      dispatch_after(dispatch_time(DISPATCH_TIME_NOW, (int64_t)(1 * NSEC_PER_SEC)),
          dispatch_get_main_queue(), ^ {
        [((UINavigationController * ) self.window.rootViewController)
            popToRootViewControllerAnimated: NO];
        [
          [((UINavigationController * ) self.window.rootViewController).viewControllers
              firstObject] performSegueWithIdentifier: @ "PAGE2_SEGUE"
          sender: self.window.rootViewController
        ];
      });
    } else {
      return NO;
    }
  } else {
    return NO;
  }
  return YES;
}
```

Integrating Amazon Pinpoint with Android Apps

To use Amazon Pinpoint with an Android app, you must integrate code that connects your app to Amazon Pinpoint. This enables the app to send event data used by the service to track user activity and gather engagement metrics.

- Setting up the AWS Mobile SDK for Android
- Initializing the Amazon Pinpoint Client
- Managing Sessions
- Registering Endpoints
- Reporting Events
- Handling Push Notifications

Setting up the AWS Mobile SDK for Android

Before modifying your app to use Amazon Pinpoint, you need to set up the AWS Mobile SDK for Android.

To set up AWS Mobile SDK for Android support in your app project

1. Copy these AWS Mobile SDK for Android .jar files into the app\libs directory of your Android Studio project:

   - aws-android-sdk-core-2.3.4.jar

   - aws-android-sdk-cognito-2.3.4.jar

   - aws-android-sdk-pinpoint-2.3.4.jar

2. Make sure your `build.gradle` file contains the following build dependencies:

```
1 compile fileTree(include: ['*.jar'], dir: 'libs')
2 compile 'com.google.firebase:firebase-messaging:9.6.0'
```

   Or you can list and compile each .jar file individually, as follows:

```
1 compile files('libs/aws-android-sdk-core-2.3.4.jar')
2 compile files('libs/aws-android-sdk-cognito-2.3.4.jar')
3 compile files('libs/aws-android-sdk-pinpoint-2.3.4.jar')
```

3. After the dependencies brackets, push:

```
1 apply plugin: 'com.google.gms.google-services'
```

Managing Sessions

As users engage with your app, it reports information about app sessions to Amazon Pinpoint, such as session start times, session end times, and events that occur during sessions. To report this information, your app must include methods that handle events as your app enters the foreground and the background on the user's Android device.

When you use AWS Mobile Hub to create a project for your Amazon Pinpoint app, Mobile Hub provides a sample app that demonstrates how to integrate with Amazon Pinpoint. The Android version of the sample app includes the `AbstractApplicationLifeCycleHelper` class to help you manage app sessions. Include this class in your Android app package.

For more information about creating the Mobile Hub sample app, see Getting Started With Android Apps.

After you include the `AbstractApplicationLifeCycleHelper` class, implement the abstract methods, `applicationEnteredForeground` and `applicationEnteredBackground`, in the `Application` file in your app package. These methods enable your app to report the following information to Amazon Pinpoint:

- Session start times (when the app enters the foreground).
- Session end times (when the app enters the background).
- The events that occur during the app session, such as monetization events. This information is reported when the app enters the background.

The following example shows how to implement the `applicationEnteredForeground` and `applicationEnteredBackground` abstract methods:

```
1  applicationLifeCycleHelper = new AbstractApplicationLifeCycleHelper(this) {
2      @Override
3      protected void applicationEnteredForeground() {
4          final PinpointManager pinpointManager = AWSMobileClient.defaultMobileClient()
5              .getPinpointManager();
6          pinpointManager.getSessionClient().startSession();
7          // Handles events that occur when your app enters the foreground.
8      }
9
10     @Override
11     protected void applicationEnteredBackground() {
12         Log.d(LOG_TAG, "Detected application has entered the background.");
13         final PinpointManager pinpointManager = AWSMobileClient.defaultMobileClient()
14             .getPinpointManager();
15         pinpointManager.getSessionClient().stopSession();
16         pinpointManager.getAnalyticsClient().submitEvents();
17         // Handles events that occur when your app enters the background.
18     }
19 };
```

Handling Push Notifications from Firebase Cloud Messaging or Google Cloud Messaging

Modify your app code to handle push notifications from Firebase Cloud Messaging (FCM) or its predecessor, Google Cloud Messaging (GCM).

Set up the Manifest File

If you are using FCM, add the following entries to your `AndroidManifest.xml` file before the `<application>` tag.

```
1  <receiver
2      android:name="com.amazonaws.mobileconnectors.pinpoint.targeting.notification.
           PinpointNotificationReceiver"
3      android:exported="false" >
4      <intent-filter>
5          <action android:name="com.amazonaws.intent.fcm.NOTIFICATION_OPEN" />
6      </intent-filter>
7  </receiver>
```

If you are using GCM, you must provide permissions for your app to register, receive, and respond to GCM notifications. Add the following entries to your `AndroidManifest.xml` file before the `<application>` tag.

```
1  <uses-permission android:name="android.permission.INTERNET" />
2  <uses-permission android:name="android.permission.ACCESS_NETWORK_STATE" />
3  <uses-permission android:name="android.permission.ACCESS_WIFI_STATE" />
4  <uses-permission android:name="android.permission.WAKE_LOCK"/>
5  <uses-permission android:name="com.google.android.c2dm.permission.RECEIVE" />
6  <permission android:name="PACKAGE_NAME.permission.C2D_MESSAGE"
7      android:protectionLevel="signature" />
8  <uses-permission android:name="PACKAGE_NAME.permission.C2D_MESSAGE" />
```

Install a listener for push notification messages from Google servers. Add the following entries to your `AndroidManifest.xml` file inside the `<application>` tag:

```
1  <receiver
2      android:name="com.google.android.gms.gcm.GcmReceiver"
3      android:exported="true"
4      android:permission="com.google.android.c2dm.permission.SEND" >
5      <intent-filter>
6          <action android:name="com.google.android.c2dm.intent.RECEIVE" />
7          <category android:name="@string/google_cloud_messaging_package" />
8      </intent-filter>
9  </receiver>
```

Register a service that extends the Google `GcmListenerService` to listen for push notifications. Here is an example of such a service called `PushListenerService`.

```
1  <service
2      android:name="PACKAGE_NAME.PushListenerService"
3      android:exported="false" >
4      <intent-filter>
5          <action android:name="com.google.android.c2dm.intent.RECEIVE" />
6      </intent-filter>
7  </service>
```

Register the Token

If you are using GCM, register the GCM token with the Amazon Pinpoint client.

In the following example, the `AWSMobileClient` class is provided in the AWS Mobile Hub sample code to reference the Amazon Pinpoint object.

```
1 InstanceID instanceID = InstanceID.getInstance(this);
2 String gcmToken =
3     instanceID.getToken(
4         getString(R.string.gcm_defaultSenderId),
5         GoogleCloudMessaging.INSTANCE_ID_SCOPE,
6         null);
7 AWSMobileClient.defaultMobileClient().getPinpointManager().getNotificationClient().
      registerGCMDeviceToken(refreshedToken) ;
```

If you are using FCM, call this object inside your class that extends `FirebaseInstanceIdService`:

```
1 /**
2  * Called if InstanceID token is updated. This may occur if the security of
3  * the previous token has been compromised. Note that this is called when the InstanceID token
4  * is initially generated so this is where you would retrieve the token.
5  */
6 // [START refresh_token]
7 @Override
8 public void onTokenRefresh() {
9     // Get updated InstanceID token.
10     String refreshedToken = FirebaseInstanceId.getInstance().getToken();
11     Log.d(TAG, "Refreshed token: " + refreshedToken);
12
13     // If you want to send messages to this application instance or
14     // manage this apps subscriptions on the server side, send the
15     // Instance ID token to your app server.
16
17     AWSMobileClient.defaultMobileClient().getPinpointManager().getNotificationClient().
          registerGCMDeviceToken(refreshedToken);
18 }
19 // [END refresh_token]
```

Handling the Message

You must add a hook to handle the message.

If you are using GCM, add a hook in the class in your app that extends `GcmListenerService` in the `onMessageReceived` method:

```
1 @Override
2 public void onMessageReceived(final String from, final Bundle data) {
3     AWSMobileClient.initializeMobileClientIfNecessary(this.getApplicationContext());
4     final NotificationClient notificationClient = AWSMobileClient.defaultMobileClient()
5         .getPinpointManager().getNotificationClient();
6
7     NotificationClient.CampaignPushResult pushResult =
8         notificationClient.handleGCMCampaignPush(from, data, this.getClass());
```

If you are using FCM, add a hook in the class in your app that extends `FirebaseMessagingService` in the `onMessageReceived` method:

```
1  /**
2      * Called when message is received.
3      *
4      * @param remoteMessage Object representing the message received from Firebase Cloud
            Messaging.
5      */
6     // [START receive_message]
7     @Override
8     public void onMessageReceived(RemoteMessage remoteMessage) {
9
10 AWSMobileClient.defaultMobileClient().getPinpointManager().getNotificationClient().
       handleFCMCampaignPush(remoteMessage.getFrom(), remoteMessage.getData());
11     }
12     // [END receive_message]
```

Handling Push Notifications from Amazon Device Messaging

Amazon Device Messaging (ADM) is a service used to send push notifications to apps running on Amazon devices, such as Kindle Fire tablets. By integrating ADM with your app, you can use Amazon Pinpoint to send notifications to your app through the ADM mobile push channel.

Prerequisites

To send push notifications to your app using Amazon Pinpoint and ADM, you need the following:
Amazon Developer account. Client ID and client secret from Amazon Device Messaging. ADM registration ID (provided by the end device that contains the ADM platform). You must also set up SDK support and initialize the Amazon Pinpoint client before you begin.

Integrating ADM with Your App

If you are already familiar with ADM and have ADM credentials, you can follow the steps for Integrating Your App with Amazon Device Messaging in the Amazon Developer documentation. Otherwise, for an introduction to ADM, see Understanding Amazon Device Messaging.

To integrate with Amazon Pinpoint, your subclass implementation of `com.amazon.device.messaging.` `ADMMessageHandlerBase` should include the following methods and perform the corresponding calls:

`onRegistered`
Called when the device is registered with the ADM service. Provides the ADM registration ID that is needed to register the device with Amazon Pinpoint. Include the following call as part of this method:

```
1 pinpointManager.getNotificationClient().registerDeviceToken(registrationId)
```

`onUnregistered`
Called when the device is no longer registered with the ADM service.

`onMessage`
Called when the device receives a message notification from ADM. Include the following as part of this method:

```
1 NotificaitonDetails details = NotificationDetailsBuilder.builder()
2                               .intent(intent);
3                               .intentAction(NotificationClient.ADM_INTENT_ACTION)
4                               .build();
5
6 pinpointManager.getNotificationClient().handleCampaignPush(details)
```

Testing ADM Push Notifications

To test, you need an Amazon Pinpoint project, an ADM client ID, and an ADM client secret.

Before you begin, augment your app to display the device token after registration. The device token can be retrieved by calling:

```
1 pinpointManager.getNotificationClient().getDeviceToken()
```

Complete the following steps using the AWS CLI.

To test ADM push notifications

1. Register ADM as a channel with your Amazon Pinpoint project. Provide the ADM client ID and the ADM client secret.

```
1 aws pinpoint update-adm-channel --application-id [YourPinpointAppId] --adm-channel-request
    "{
2     \"ClientId\": \"ADM_CLIENT_ID",
3     \"Enabled\": true,
4     \"ClientSecret\": \"ADM_CLIENT_SECRET"
5 }"
```

2. Install your app on a device that has ADM enabled, and capture the generated device token.

3. Send a direct message to the device specifying the device token as the address.

```
1 aws pinpoint send-messages --application-id YourPinpointAppId --message-request "{
2   \"Addresses\": {
3       \"DeviceToken\": {
4           \"ChannelType\": \"ADM\"
5       }
6   },
7   \"MessageConfiguration\": {
8       \"ADMMessage\": {
9           \"RawContent\":\"{'pinpoint.campaign.campaign_id':'_DIRECT','pinpoint.
                notification.silentPush':0,'pinpoint.openApp':true,'pinpoint.notification.
                title':'Hello','pinpoint.notification.body':'Hello World.'}\"
10      }
11  }
12 }"
```

Handling Push Notifications from Baidu Cloud Push

Baidu Cloud Push is the push notification service provided by Baidu, a Chinese cloud service. By integrating Baidu Cloud Push with your mobile app, you can use Amazon Pinpoint to send notifications to your app through the Baidu mobile push channel.

Prerequisites

To send push notifications to mobile devices using Amazon Pinpoint and Baidu, you need the following: Baidu account. Registration as a Baidu developer. Baidu Cloud Push project. API key and secret key from a Baidu Cloud Push project. Baidu user ID and channel ID. You must also set up SDK support and initialize the Amazon Pinpoint client before you begin.

Integrating Baidu Cloud Push with Your App

The following procedure is based on version 5.7.1.65 of the Baidu push service jar.

To integrate Baidu with your app

1. Download the latest Baidu Cloud Push SDK Android client from http://push.baidu.com/.

2. Extract the zip file and import the `pushservice-x.x.xx.jar` file from the Baidu-Push-SDK-Android `libs` folder into your Android app's `lib` folder.

3. The Baidu-Push-SDK-Android `libs` folder should also include the following folders:

   - `arm64-v8a/`

   - `armeabi/`

   - `armeabi-v7a/`

   - `mips/`

   - `mips64/`

   - `x86/`

   - `x86_64/`

   Add each complete folder to your Android app's `src/main/jniLibs` folder.

4. In the Android app's `AndroidManifest.xml` file, declare the following permissions:

```
1  <uses-permission android:name="android.permission.INTERNET" />
2  <uses-permission android:name="android.permission.ACCESS_NETWORK_STATE" />
3  <uses-permission android:name="android.permission.ACCESS_WIFI_STATE" />
4
5  <!-- Baidu permissions -->
6  <uses-permission android:name="android.permission.WAKE_LOCK"/>
7  <uses-permission android:name="com.google.android.c2dm.permission.RECEIVE" />
8
9  <uses-permission android:name="android.permission.READ_PHONE_STATE" />
10 <uses-permission android:name="android.permission.RECEIVE_BOOT_COMPLETED" />
11 <uses-permission android:name="android.permission.WRITE_SETTINGS" />
12 <uses-permission android:name="android.permission.VIBRATE" />
13 <uses-permission android:name="android.permission.WRITE_EXTERNAL_STORAGE" />
14 <uses-permission android:name="android.permission.ACCESS_DOWNLOAD_MANAGER" />
15 <uses-permission android:name="android.permission.DOWNLOAD_WITHOUT_NOTIFICATION" />
16 <uses-permission android:name="android.permission.DISABLE_KEYGUARD" />
```

5. Under `<application>`, specify the following receivers and intent filters:

```
1  <!-- Baidu settings -->
2  <receiver android:name="com.baidu.android.pushservice.PushServiceReceiver"
3            android:process=":bdservice_v1">
4    <intent-filter>
5      <action android:name="android.intent.action.BOOT_COMPLETED" />
6      <action android:name="android.net.conn.CONNECTIVITY_CHANGE" />
7      <action android:name="com.baidu.android.pushservice.action.notification.SHOW" />
8      <action android:name="com.baidu.android.pushservice.action.media.CLICK" />
9      <!-- actionservice -->
10     <action android:name="android.intent.action.MEDIA_MOUNTED" />
11     <action android:name="android.intent.action.USER_PRESENT" />
12     <action android:name="android.intent.action.ACTION_POWER_CONNECTED" />
13     <action android:name="android.intent.action.ACTION_POWER_DISCONNECTED" />
14   </intent-filter>
15 </receiver>
16 <receiver
17           android:name="com.baidu.android.pushservice.RegistrationReceiver"
18           android:process=":bdservice_v1">
19   <intent-filter>
20     <action android:name="com.baidu.android.pushservice.action.METHOD" />
21     <action android:name="com.baidu.android.pushservice.action.BIND_SYNC" />
22   </intent-filter>
23   <intent-filter>
24     <action android:name="android.intent.action.PACKAGE_REMOVED" />
25
26     <data android:scheme="package" />
27   </intent-filter>
28 </receiver>
29
30 <service
31           android:name="com.baidu.android.pushservice.PushService"
32           android:exported="true"
33           android:process=":bdservice_v1">
34   <intent-filter>
35     <action android:name="com.baidu.android.pushservice.action.PUSH_SERVICE" />
36   </intent-filter>
37 </service>
38 <service
39           android:name="com.baidu.android.pushservice.CommandService"
40           android:exported="true" />
41 <!-- Amazon Pinpoint Notification Receiver -->
42 <receiver android:name="com.amazonaws.mobileconnectors.pinpoint.targeting.notification.
     PinpointNotificationReceiver">
43   <intent-filter>
44   <action android:name="com.amazonaws.intent.baidu.NOTIFICATION_OPEN" />
45   </intent-filter>
46 </receiver>
```

6. Update the `AndroidManifest.xml` file with the following permissions, which are specific to your application. Remember to replace *YourPackageName* with the name of your package.

```
1 <!-- Android NContentProvider-->
2 <uses-permission android:name="baidu.push.permission.WRITE_PUSHINFOPROVIDER.YourPackageName
     " />
3 <permission
```

```
4           android:name="baidu.push.permission.WRITE_PUSHINFOPROVIDER.YourPackageName"
5           android:protectionLevel="normal"></permission>
6 <!-- Android NContentProvider-->
7 <provider
8           android:name="com.baidu.android.pushservice.PushInfoProvider"
9           android:authorities="YourPackageName.bdpush"
10          android:exported="true"
11          android:protectionLevel="signature"
12          android:writePermission="baidu.push.permission.WRITE_PUSHINFOPROVIDER.
               YourPackageName" />
```

7. Inside your Android application, create a `MessageReceiver` class that subclasses `com.baidu.android.pushservice.PushMessageReceiver`. The subclass should implement the following methods and perform the corresponding calls:

`onBind`
Called when the device is registered with Baidu Cloud Push. Provides the Baidu user ID and channel ID that are needed to register the device with Amazon Pinpoint. Include the following call as part of this method:

```
1 pinpointManager.getNotificationClient().registerDeviceToken(registrationId)
```

`onUnbind`
Called when the device is no longer registered with Baidu Cloud Push.

`onMessage`
Called when the device receives a raw message from Baidu Cloud Push. Amazon Pinpoint transmits campaign push notifications with the Baidu Cloud Push raw message format. Include the following call as part of this method:

```
1 NotificaitonDetails details = NotificationDetailsBuilder.builder()
2                               .message(message);
3                               .intentAction(NotificationClient.BAIDU_INTENT_ACTION)
4                               .build();
5
6 pinpointManager.getNotificationClient().handleCampaignPush(details)
```

Only the message parameter contains data. The `customContentString` is not used with raw messages.

1. After creating the subclass, modify the `AndoriodManifest.xml` file to register it as a receiver. In the following example, the `PushMessageReceiver` subclass is named `com.baidu.push.example.MyPushMessageReceiver`.

```
1 <!-- pushreceiver -->
2 <receiver android:name="com.baidu.push.example.MyPushMessageReceiver">
3   <intent-filter>
4     <!-- push -->
5     <action android:name="com.baidu.android.pushservice.action.MESSAGE" />
6     <!-- bind,unbind,fetch,delete -->
7     <action android:name="com.baidu.android.pushservice.action.RECEIVE" />
8     <action android:name="com.baidu.android.pushservice.action.notification.CLICK" />
9   </intent-filter>
10 </receiver>
```

2. To start the Baidu listener service, in your Android app's main activity, add the following code to the `onCreate` method:

```
1 // Push: apikeyActivityonCreate
2 //   ATTENTIONYou need to modify the value of api_key to your own !!
```

71

```
3 // push
4 PushManager.startWork(getApplicationContext(), PushConstants.LOGIN_TYPE_API_KEY, api_key);
5
6 // Push: API
7 // ->->1
8 //  PushManager.setNotificationBuilder(this, 1, cBuilder)
9 CustomPushNotificationBuilder cBuilder = new CustomPushNotificationBuilder(
10  getResources().getIdentifier("notification_custom_builder", "layout", getPackageName()),
11  getResources().getIdentifier("notification_icon", "id", getPackageName()),
12  getResources().getIdentifier("notification_title", "id", getPackageName()),
13  getResources().getIdentifier("notification_text", "id", getPackageName()));
14 cBuilder.setNotificationFlags(Notification.FLAG_AUTO_CANCEL);
15 cBuilder.setNotificationDefaults(Notification.DEFAULT_VIBRATE);
16
17 cBuilder.setStatusbarIcon(this.getApplicationInfo().icon);
18 cBuilder.setLayoutDrawable(getResources().getIdentifier(
19  "simple_notification_icon", "drawable", getPackageName()));
20 cBuilder.setNotificationSound(Uri.withAppendedPath(
21  Audio.Media.INTERNAL_CONTENT_URI, "6").toString());
22 // ID
23 PushManager.setNotificationBuilder(this, 1, cBuilder);
```

3. Remember to properly initialize your `PinpointManager` reference. Use a `PinpointConfiguration` with a `ChannelType` value of `ChannelType.BAIDU`. You can do this programmatically, as in the following example:

```
1 final PinpointConfiguration config =
2   new PinpointConfiguration(this,
3                             IdentityManager.getDefaultIdentityManager()
4                             .getCredentialsProvider(),
5                             awsConfiguration)
6   .withChannelType(ChannelType.BAIDU);
7 Application.pinpointManager = new PinpointManager(config);
```

Or, you can define a configuration file to be consumed by `AWSConfiguration`:

```
1 "PinpointAnalytics": {
2    "Default": {
3      "AppId": "[YourPinpointAppId]",
4      "Region": "us-east-1",
5      "ChannelType": "BAIDU"
6    }
7  }
```

Testing Baidu Push Notifications

To test, you need an Amazon Pinpoint project, a Baidu API key, and a Baidu Secret key.

Before you begin, augment your app to display the device token after registration. The device token can be retrieved by calling:

```
1 PinpointManager::getNotificationClient().getDeviceToken()
```

Complete the following steps using the AWS CLI.

To test Baidu push notifications

1. Register Baidu as a channel with your Amazon Pinpoint project. Provide the Baidu API key and Secret key.

```
1 aws pinpoint update-baidu-channel --application-id YourPinpointAppId --baidu-channel-
      request "{
2   \"ApiKey\": \"BAIDU_API_KEY\",
3   \"Enabled\": true,
4   \"SecretKey\": \"BAIDU_SECRET_KEY\"
5 }"
```

2. Install your app on to a Baidu-enabled device and capture the generated device token.

3. Send a direct message to the device specifying the device token as the address.

```
1 aws pinpoint send-messages --application-id YourPinpointAppId --message-request "{
2   \"Addresses\": {
3       \"DeviceToken\": {
4           \"ChannelType\": \"BAIDU\"
5       }
6   },
7   \"MessageConfiguration\": {
8       \"BaiduMessage\": {
9           \"RawContent\":\"{'pinpoint.campaign.campaign_id':'_DIRECT','pinpoint.
              notification.silentPush':0,'pinpoint.openApp':true,'pinpoint.notification.
              title':'Hello','pinpoint.notification.body':'Hello World.'}\"
10      }
11  }
12 }"
```

Setting up Deep Linking

Amazon Pinpoint campaigns can take one of three actions when a user taps a notification. One of those possible actions is a deep link, which opens the app to a specified activity.

To specify a destination activity for deep links, the app must have set up deep linking. This setup requires an intent filter that registers a URL scheme the deep links will use. After the app creates an intent filter, the data provided by the intent determines the activity to render.

Creating an Intent Filter

Begin to set up deep linking by creating an intent filter in your `AndroidManifest.xml` file. For example:

```
1  <!-- This activity allows your application to receive a deep link that navigates directly to the
2  "Deeplink Page"-->
3  <activity
4      android:name=".DeepLinkActivity"
5      android:label="A deeplink!" >
6      <intent-filter android:label="inAppReceiver">
7          <action android:name="android.intent.action.VIEW" />
8          <category android:name="android.intent.category.DEFAULT" />
9          <category android:name="android.intent.category.BROWSABLE" />
10         <!-- Accepts URIs of type "pinpoint://deeplink" -->
11         <data android:scheme="pinpoint"
12             android:host="deeplink" />
13     </intent-filter>
14 </activity>
```

The data element in the previous example registers a URL scheme, `pinpoint://`, as well as the host, `deeplink`. As a result, when given a URL in the form of `pinpoint://deeplink`, the manifest is prepared to execute the action.

Handling the Intent

Next, set up an intent handler to present the screen associated with the registered URL scheme and host. Intent data is retrieved in the `onCreate()` method, which then can use `Uri data` to create an activity. The following example shows an alert and tracks an event.

```
1  public class DeeplinkActivity extends Activity {
2
3      public void onCreate(Bundle savedInstanceState) {
4          super.onCreate(savedInstanceState);
5
6          if (getIntent().getAction() == Intent.ACTION_VIEW) {
7              Uri data = getIntent().getData();
8
9              if (data != null) {
10
11                 // show an alert with the "custom" param
12                 new AlertDialog.Builder(this)
13                         .setTitle("An example of a Deeplink")
14                         .setMessage("Found custom param: " +data.getQueryParameter("custom"))
15                         .setPositiveButton(android.R.string.yes, new DialogInterface.
                               OnClickListener() {
```

```
16              public void onClick(DialogInterface dialog, int which) {
17                  dialog.dismiss();
18              }
19          })
20          .setIcon(android.R.drawable.ic_dialog_alert)
21          .show();
22      }
23  }
24  }
25 }
```

Adding Endpoints

An *endpoint* is a unique messaging destination. When you send messages using Amazon Pinpoint, you send them to endpoints. Examples of endpoints include email addresses, mobile phone numbers, and mobile device identifiers.

You can add attributes to endpoints to better describe your users. After you add endpoints to Amazon Pinpoint, you can create segments based on customer attributes, and then engage with your segments by sending tailored messages.

You can associate endpoints with user IDs to identify individual users. You can also associate multiple endpoints with a single user ID.

If you're a mobile developer and you've integrated Amazon Pinpoint into your app, your app automatically registers an endpoint with Amazon Pinpoint when a new user opens it, and updates existing endpoints when returning users open it. You can also add endpoints programmatically by using the Amazon Pinpoint API or an AWS SDK.

For more information, see Endpoints in the *Amazon Pinpoint API Reference*.

Adding Endpoints Programmatically

The following example demonstrates how to add endpoints to Amazon Pinpoint programmatically by using the AWS SDK for Java.

```java
1  import com.amazonaws.services.pinpoint.AmazonPinpointClient;
2  import com.amazonaws.services.pinpoint.model.EndpointDemographic;
3  import com.amazonaws.services.pinpoint.model.EndpointLocation;
4  import com.amazonaws.services.pinpoint.model.EndpointRequest;
5  import com.amazonaws.services.pinpoint.model.EndpointResponse;
6  import com.amazonaws.services.pinpoint.model.EndpointUser;
7  import com.amazonaws.services.pinpoint.model.GetEndpointRequest;
8  import com.amazonaws.services.pinpoint.model.GetEndpointResult;
9  import com.amazonaws.services.pinpoint.model.UpdateEndpointRequest;
10 import com.amazonaws.services.pinpoint.model.UpdateEndpointResult;
11
12 import java.util.ArrayList;
13 import java.util.Date;
14 import java.util.HashMap;
15 import java.util.List;
16 import java.util.Map;
17 import java.util.UUID;
18
19 public class PinpointEndpointSample {
20
21     public EndpointResponse createEndpoint(AmazonPinpointClient client, String appId) {
22         String endpointId = UUID.randomUUID().toString();
23         System.out.println("Endpoint ID: " + endpointId);
24
25         EndpointRequest endpointRequest = createEndpointRequestData();
26
27         UpdateEndpointRequest updateEndpointRequest = new UpdateEndpointRequest()
28                 .withApplicationId(appId)
29                 .withEndpointId(endpointId)
30                 .withEndpointRequest(endpointRequest);
31
```

```java
32    UpdateEndpointResult updateEndpointResponse = client.updateEndpoint(
         updateEndpointRequest);
33    System.out.println("Update Endpoint Response: " + updateEndpointResponse.getMessageBody
         ());
34
35    GetEndpointRequest getEndpointRequest = new GetEndpointRequest()
36          .withApplicationId(appId)
37          .withEndpointId(endpointId);
38    GetEndpointResult getEndpointResult = client.getEndpoint(getEndpointRequest);
39
40    System.out.println("Got Endpoint: " + getEndpointResult.getEndpointResponse().getId());
41    return getEndpointResult.getEndpointResponse();
42 }
43
44 private EndpointRequest createEndpointRequestData() {
45
46    HashMap<String, List<String>> customAttributes = new HashMap<>();
47    List<String> favoriteTeams = new ArrayList<>();
48    favoriteTeams.add("Lakers");
49    favoriteTeams.add("Warriors");
50    customAttributes.put("team", favoriteTeams);
51
52
53    EndpointDemographic demographic = new EndpointDemographic()
54          .withAppVersion("1.0")
55          .withMake("apple")
56          .withModel("iPhone")
57          .withModelVersion("7")
58          .withPlatform("ios")
59          .withPlatformVersion("10.1.1")
60          .withTimezone("Americas/Los_Angeles");
61
62    EndpointLocation location = new EndpointLocation()
63          .withCity("Los Angeles")
64          .withCountry("US")
65          .withLatitude(34.0)
66          .withLongitude(-118.2)
67          .withPostalCode("90068")
68          .withRegion("CA");
69
70    Map<String,Double> metrics = new HashMap<>();
71    metrics.put("health", 100.00);
72    metrics.put("luck", 75.00);
73
74    EndpointUser user = new EndpointUser()
75          .withUserId(UUID.randomUUID().toString());
76
77    EndpointRequest endpointRequest = new EndpointRequest()
78          .withAddress(UUID.randomUUID().toString())
79          .withAttributes(customAttributes)
80          .withChannelType("APNS")
81          .withDemographic(demographic)
82          .withEffectiveDate(new Date().toString())
83          .withLocation(location)
```

```
84                    .withMetrics(metrics)
85                    .withOptOut("NONE")
86                    .withRequestId(UUID.randomUUID().toString())
87                    .withUser(user);
88
89        return endpointRequest;
90    }
91 }
```

When you run this example, the following is printed to the console window of your IDE.

```
1 Endpoint ID: 37d321e8-5419-4fa8-86ba-698905f262a4
2 Update Endpoint Response: {Message: Accepted,RequestID: 74ef5959-b4d7-11e6-ae27-25eb3a23dee7}
3 Get Endpoint ID: 37d321e8-5419-4fa8-86ba-698905f262a4
```

Creating Segments

A user *segment* represents a subset of your users based on shared characteristics, such as how recently the users have used your app or which device platform they use. A segment designates which users receive the messages delivered by a campaign. Define segments so that you can reach the right audience when you want to invite users back to your app, make special offers, or otherwise increase user engagement and purchasing.

After you create a segment, you can use it in one or more campaigns. A campaign delivers tailored messages to the users in the segment.

For more information, see Segments.

- Building Segments
- Importing Segments
- Customizing Segments with AWS Lambda

Building Segments

To reach the intended audience for a campaign, build a segment based on the data reported by your app. For example, to reach users who haven't used your app recently, you can define a segment for users who haven't used your app in the last 7 days.

Building Segments With the AWS SDK for Java

The following example demonstrates how to build a segment with the AWS SDK for Java.

```
1  import com.amazonaws.services.pinpoint.AmazonPinpointClient;
2  import com.amazonaws.services.pinpoint.model.AttributeDimension;
3  import com.amazonaws.services.pinpoint.model.AttributeType;
4  import com.amazonaws.services.pinpoint.model.CreateSegmentRequest;
5  import com.amazonaws.services.pinpoint.model.CreateSegmentResult;
6  import com.amazonaws.services.pinpoint.model.RecencyDimension;
7  import com.amazonaws.services.pinpoint.model.SegmentBehaviors;
8  import com.amazonaws.services.pinpoint.model.SegmentDemographics;
9  import com.amazonaws.services.pinpoint.model.SegmentDimensions;
10 import com.amazonaws.services.pinpoint.model.SegmentLocation;
11 import com.amazonaws.services.pinpoint.model.SegmentResponse;
12 import com.amazonaws.services.pinpoint.model.WriteSegmentRequest;
13
14 import java.util.HashMap;
15 import java.util.Map;
16
17 public class PinpointSegmentSample {
18
19     public SegmentResponse createSegment(AmazonPinpointClient client, String appId) {
20         Map<String, AttributeDimension> segmentAttributes = new HashMap<>();
21         segmentAttributes.put("Team", new AttributeDimension().withAttributeType(AttributeType.
                INCLUSIVE).withValues("Lakers"));
22
23         SegmentBehaviors segmentBehaviors = new SegmentBehaviors();
24         SegmentDemographics segmentDemographics = new SegmentDemographics();
25         SegmentLocation segmentLocation = new SegmentLocation();
26
27         RecencyDimension recencyDimension = new RecencyDimension();
28         recencyDimension.withDuration("DAY_30").withRecencyType("ACTIVE");
29         segmentBehaviors.setRecency(recencyDimension);
30
31         SegmentDimensions dimensions = new SegmentDimensions()
32                 .withAttributes(segmentAttributes)
33                 .withBehavior(segmentBehaviors)
34                 .withDemographic(segmentDemographics)
35                 .withLocation(segmentLocation);
36
37
38         WriteSegmentRequest writeSegmentRequest = new WriteSegmentRequest()
39                 .withName("MySegment").withDimensions(dimensions);
40
41         CreateSegmentRequest createSegmentRequest = new CreateSegmentRequest()
42                 .withApplicationId(appId).withWriteSegmentRequest(writeSegmentRequest);
43
```

```
44        CreateSegmentResult createSegmentResult = client.createSegment(createSegmentRequest);
45
46        System.out.println("Segment ID: " + createSegmentResult.getSegmentResponse().getId());
47
48        return createSegmentResult.getSegmentResponse();
49    }
50
51 }
```

When you run this example, the following is printed to the console window of your IDE:

```
1 Segment ID: 09cb2967a82b4a2fbab38fead8d1f4c4
```

Importing Segments

With Amazon Pinpoint, you can define a user segment by importing information about the endpoints that belong to the segment. An *endpoint* is a single messaging destination, such as a mobile push device token, a mobile phone number, or an email address.

Importing segments is useful if you've already created segments of your users outside of Amazon Pinpoint but you want to engage your users with Amazon Pinpoint campaigns.

When you import a segment, Amazon Pinpoint gets the segment's endpoints from Amazon Simple Storage Service (Amazon S3). Before you import, you add the endpoints to Amazon S3, and you create an IAM role that grants Amazon Pinpoint access to Amazon S3. Then, you give Amazon Pinpoint the Amazon S3 location where the endpoints are stored, and Amazon Pinpoint adds each endpoint to the segment.

To create the IAM role, see IAM Role for Importing Segments. For information about importing a segment by using the Amazon Pinpoint console, see Importing Segments in the *Amazon Pinpoint User Guide*.

Importing a Segment

The following example demonstrates how to import a segment by using the AWS SDK for Java.

```
1  import com.amazonaws.services.pinpoint.AmazonPinpointClient;
2  import com.amazonaws.services.pinpoint.model.AttributeDimension;
3  import com.amazonaws.services.pinpoint.model.AttributeType;
4  import com.amazonaws.services.pinpoint.model.CreateImportJobRequest;
5  import com.amazonaws.services.pinpoint.model.CreateImportJobResult;
6  import com.amazonaws.services.pinpoint.model.CreateSegmentRequest;
7  import com.amazonaws.services.pinpoint.model.CreateSegmentResult;
8  import com.amazonaws.services.pinpoint.model.Format;
9  import com.amazonaws.services.pinpoint.model.GetImportJobRequest;
10 import com.amazonaws.services.pinpoint.model.GetImportJobResult;
11 import com.amazonaws.services.pinpoint.model.GetSegmentRequest;
12 import com.amazonaws.services.pinpoint.model.GetSegmentResult;
13 import com.amazonaws.services.pinpoint.model.ImportJobRequest;
14 import com.amazonaws.services.pinpoint.model.JobStatus;
15 import com.amazonaws.services.pinpoint.model.RecencyDimension;
16 import com.amazonaws.services.pinpoint.model.SegmentBehaviors;
17 import com.amazonaws.services.pinpoint.model.SegmentDemographics;
18 import com.amazonaws.services.pinpoint.model.SegmentDimensions;
19 import com.amazonaws.services.pinpoint.model.SegmentLocation;
20 import com.amazonaws.services.pinpoint.model.SegmentResponse;
21 import com.amazonaws.services.pinpoint.model.WriteSegmentRequest;
22
23 import java.util.HashMap;
24 import java.util.Map;
25
26 public class PinpointImportSample {
27
28     public SegmentResponse createImportSegment(AmazonPinpointClient client, String appId,
29                                     String bucket, String key,
30                                     String roleArn) throws Exception {
31
32         // Create the job.
33         ImportJobRequest importRequest = new ImportJobRequest()
34                 .withDefineSegment(true)
```

```
35              .withRegisterEndpoints(true)
36              .withRoleArn(roleArn)
37              .withFormat(Format.JSON)
38              .withS3Url("s3://" + bucket + "/" + key);
39
40      CreateImportJobRequest jobRequest = new CreateImportJobRequest()
41              .withImportJobRequest(importRequest)
42              .withApplicationId(appId);
43
44      CreateImportJobResult jobResponse = client.createImportJob(jobRequest);
45
46      GetImportJobRequest fetchRequest = new GetImportJobRequest()
47              .withApplicationId(appId)
48              .withJobId(jobResponse.getImportJobResponse().getId());
49
50      // Wait for job to finish.
51
52      GetImportJobResult getJobResponse;
53
54      do {
55          // Lets only check once every 10 seconds if done, busy waits are bad.
56
57          Thread.sleep(10 * 1000);
58
59          getJobResponse = client.getImportJob(fetchRequest);
60
61          if (getJobResponse.getImportJobResponse().getJobStatus().equals(JobStatus.FAILED)) {
62              throw new Exception("Failed to process import job successfully");
63          }
64      } while(!getJobResponse.getImportJobResponse().getJobStatus().equals(JobStatus.COMPLETED
           ));
65
66      // Finally get the import segment that was created.
67
68      GetSegmentRequest segmentRequest = new GetSegmentRequest()
69              .withApplicationId(appId)
70              .withSegmentId(getJobResponse.getImportJobResponse().getId());
71
72      GetSegmentResult getSegmentResult = client.getSegment(segmentRequest);
73
74      // Print out what we got
75
76      System.out.println("Segment ID: " + getSegmentResult.getSegmentResponse().getId()
77              + " with size " + getSegmentResult.getSegmentResponse().getImportDefinition().
                 getSize());
78
79      return getSegmentResult.getSegmentResponse();
80  }
81
82 }
```

Customizing Segments with AWS Lambda

This is prerelease documentation for a feature in public beta release. It is subject to change.

You can use AWS Lambda to tailor how an Amazon Pinpoint campaign engages your target audience. With AWS Lambda, you can modify the campaign's segment at the moment that Amazon Pinpoint delivers the campaign's message.

AWS Lambda is a compute service that you can use to run code without provisioning or managing servers. You package your code and upload it to Lambda as *Lambda functions*. Lambda runs a function when the function is invoked, which might be done manually by you or automatically in response to events.

For more information, see Lambda Functions in the *AWS Lambda Developer Guide*.

To assign a Lambda function to a campaign, you define the campaign's http://docs.aws.amazon.com/pinpoint/latest/apireference/rest-api-campaign.html#rest-api-campaign-attributes-campaignhook-table settings. These settings include the Lambda function name. They also include the `CampaignHook` mode, which sets whether Amazon Pinpoint receives a return value from the function.

A Lambda function that you assign to a campaign is referred to as an Amazon Pinpoint *extension*.

With the `CampaignHook` settings defined, Amazon Pinpoint automatically invokes the Lambda function when it runs the campaign, before it delivers the campaign's message. When Amazon Pinpoint invokes the function, it provides *event data* about the message delivery. This data includes the campaign's segment, which is the list of endpoints that Amazon Pinpoint sends the message to.

If the `CampaignHook` mode is set to `FILTER`, Amazon Pinpoint allows the function to modify and return the segment before sending the message. For example, the function might update the endpoint definitions with attributes that contain data from a source that is external to Amazon Pinpoint. Or, the function might filter the segment by removing certain endpoints, based on conditions in your function code. After Amazon Pinpoint receives the modified segment from your function, it sends the message to each of the segment's endpoints using the campaign's delivery channel.

By processing your segments with AWS Lambda, you have more control over who you send messages to and what those messages contain. You can tailor your campaigns in real time, at the moment campaign messages are delivered. Filtering segments enables you to engage more narrowly defined subsets of your segments. Adding or updating endpoint attributes enables you to make new data available for message variables.

For more information about message variables, see Message Variables in the *Amazon Pinpoint User Guide*.

Note
You can also use the `CampaignHook` settings to assign a Lambda function that handles the message delivery. This type of function is useful for delivering messages through custom channels that Amazon Pinpoint doesn't support, such as social media platforms. For more information, see Creating Custom Channels with AWS Lambda.

To modify campaign segments with AWS Lambda, first create a function that processes the event data sent by Amazon Pinpoint and returns a modified segment. Then, authorize Amazon Pinpoint to invoke the function by assigning a Lambda function policy. Finally, assign the function to one or more campaigns by defining `CampaignHook` settings.

Event Data

When Amazon Pinpoint invokes your Lambda function, it provides the following payload as the event data:

```
1  {
2    "MessageConfiguration": {Message configuration}
```

```
 3    "ApplicationId": ApplicationId,
 4    "CampaignId": CampaignId,
 5    "TreatmentId": TreatmentId,
 6    "ActivityId": ActivityId,
 7    "ScheduledTime": Scheduled Time,
 8    "Endpoints": {
 9      EndpointId: {Endpoint definition}
10      . . .
11    }
12  }
```

The event data is passed to your function code by AWS Lambda.

The event data provides the following attributes:

- `MessageConfiguration` – Has the same structure as the http://docs.aws.amazon.com/pinpoint/latest/apireference/rest-api-messages.html#rest-api-messages-attributes-directmessageconfiguration-table in the `Messages` resource in the Amazon Pinpoint API.

- `ApplicationId` – The ID of the Amazon Pinpoint project that the campaign belongs to.

- `CampaignId` – The ID of the Amazon Pinpoint project that the function is invoked for.

- `TreatmentId` – The ID of a campaign variation that's used for A/B testing.

- `ActivityId` – The ID of the activity that's being performed by the campaign.

- `ScheduledTime` – The date and time when the campaign's messages will be delivered in ISO 8601 format.

- `Endpoints` – A map that associates endpoint IDs with endpoint definitions. Each event data payload contains up to 50 endpoints. If the campaign segment contains more than 50 endpoints, Amazon Pinpoint invokes the function repeatedly, with up to 50 endpoints at a time, until all endpoints have been processed.

Creating a Lambda Function

To create a Lambda function, see Building Lambda Functions in the *AWS Lambda Developer Guide*.

When you create your function, remember that the message delivery fails in the following conditions:

- The Lambda function takes longer than 15 seconds to return the modified segment.

- Amazon Pinpoint cannot decode the function's return value.

- The function requires more than 3 attempts from Amazon Pinpoint to successfully invoke.

Amazon Pinpoint only accepts endpoint definitions in the function's return value. The function cannot modify other elements in the event data.

Example Lambda Function

Your Lambda function processes the event data sent by Amazon Pinpoint, and it returns the modified endpoints, as shown by the following example handler, written in Node.js:

```
1  'use strict';
2
3  exports.handler = (event, context, callback) => {
4      for (var key in event.Endpoints) {
5          if (event.Endpoints.hasOwnProperty(key)) {
6              var endpoint = event.Endpoints[key];
7              var attr = endpoint.Attributes;
```

```
 8          if (!attr) {
 9              attr = {};
10              endpoint.Attributes = attr;
11          }
12          attr["CreditScore"] = [ Math.floor(Math.random() * 200) + 650];
13       }
14    }
15    console.log("Received event:", JSON.stringify(event, null, 2));
16    callback(null, event.Endpoints);
17 };
```

Lambda passes the event data to the handler as the `event` parameter.

In this example, the handler iterates through each endpoint in the `event.Endpoints` object, and it adds a new attribute, `CreditScore`, to the endpoint. The value of the `CreditScore` attribute is simply a random number.

The `console.log()` statement logs the event in CloudWatch Logs.

The `callback()` statement returns the modified endpoints to Amazon Pinpoint. Normally, the `callback` parameter is optional in Node.js Lambda functions, but it is required in this context because the function must return the updated endpoints to Amazon Pinpoint.

Your function must return endpoints in the same format provided by the event data, which is a map that associates endpoint IDs with endpoint definitions, as in the following example:

```
 1 {
 2     "eqmj8wpxszeqy/b3vch04sn41yw": {
 3         "ChannelType": "GCM",
 4         "Address": "4d5e6f1a2b3c4d5e6f7g8h9i0j1a2b3c",
 5         "EndpointStatus": "ACTIVE",
 6         "OptOut": "NONE",
 7         "Demographic": {
 8             "Make": "android"
 9         },
10         "EffectiveDate": "2017-11-02T21:26:48.598Z",
11         "User": {}
12     },
13     "idrexqqtn8sbwfex0ouscod0yto": {
14         "ChannelType": "APNS",
15         "Address": "1a2b3c4d5e6f7g8h9i0j1a2b3c4d5e6f",
16         "EndpointStatus": "ACTIVE",
17         "OptOut": "NONE",
18         "Demographic": {
19             "Make": "apple"
20         },
21         "EffectiveDate": "2017-11-02T21:26:48.598Z",
22         "User": {}
23     }
24 }
```

The example function modifies and returns the `event.Endpoints` object that it received in the event data.

In the endpoint definitions that you return, Amazon Pinpoint accepts `TitleOverride` and `BodyOverride` attributes.

Assigning a Lambda Function Policy

Before you can use your Lambda function to process your endpoints, you must authorize Amazon Pinpoint to invoke your Lambda function. To grant invocation permission, assign a *Lambda function policy* to the function. A Lambda function policy is a resource-based permissions policy that designates which entities can use your function and what actions those entities can take.

For more information, see Using Resource-Based Policies for AWS Lambda (Lambda Function Policies) in the *AWS Lambda Developer Guide.*

Example Function Policy

The following policy grants permission to the Amazon Pinpoint service principal to use the `lambda: InvokeFunction` action:

```
1  {
2    "Sid": "sid",
3    "Effect": "Allow",
4    "Principal": {
5      "Service": "pinpoint.us-east-1.amazonaws.com"
6    },
7    "Action": "lambda:InvokeFunction",
8    "Resource": "{arn:aws:lambda:us-east-1:account-id:function:function-name}",
9    "Condition": {
10     "ArnLike": {
11       "AWS:SourceArn": "arn:aws:mobiletargeting:us-east-1:account-id:/apps/application-id/
              campaigns/campaign-id"
12     }
13   }
14 }
```

Your function policy requires a `Condition` block that includes an `AWS:SourceArn` key. This code states which Amazon Pinpoint campaign is allowed to invoke the function. In this example, the policy grants permission to only a single campaign ID. To write a more generic policy, use multi-character match wildcards (*). For example, you can use the following `Condition` block to allow any Amazon Pinpoint campaign in your AWS account to invoke the function:

```
1  "Condition": {
2    "ArnLike": {
3      "AWS:SourceArn": "arn:aws:mobiletargeting:us-east-1:account-id:/apps/*"
4    }
5  }
```

Granting Amazon Pinpoint Invocation Permission

You can use the AWS Command Line Interface (AWS CLI) to add permissions to the Lambda function policy assigned to your Lambda function. To allow Amazon Pinpoint to invoke a function, use the Lambda http://docs.aws.amazon.com/cli/latest/reference/lambda/add-permission.html command, as shown by the following example:

```
1  $ aws lambda add-permission \
2  > --function-name function-name \
3  > --statement-id sid \
4  > --action lambda:InvokeFunction \
5  > --principal pinpoint.us-east-1.amazonaws.com \
```

```
6  > --source-arn arn:aws:mobiletargeting:us-east-1:account-id:/apps/application-id/campaigns/
     campaign-id
```

If you want to provide a campaign ID for the `--source-arn` parameter, you can look up your campaign IDs by using the Amazon Pinpoint http://docs.aws.amazon.com/cli/latest/reference/pinpoint/get-campaigns.html command with the AWS CLI. This command requires an `--application-id` parameter. To look up your application IDs, sign in to the Amazon Pinpoint console at https://console.aws.amazon.com/pinpoint/, and go to the **Projects** page. The console shows an **ID** for each project, which is the project's application ID.

When you run the Lambda `add-permission` command, AWS Lambda returns the following output:

```
1  {
2    "Statement": "{\"Sid\":\"sid\",
3     \"Effect\":\"Allow\",
4     \"Principal\":{\"Service\":\"pinpoint.us-east-1.amazonaws.com\"},
5     \"Action\":\"lambda:InvokeFunction\",
6     \"Resource\":\"arn:aws:lambda:us-east-1:111122223333:function:function-name\",
7     \"Condition\":
8       {\"ArnLike\":
9         {\"AWS:SourceArn\":
10          \"arn:aws:mobiletargeting:us-east-1:111122223333:/apps/application-id/campaigns/
             campaign-id\"}}}"
11 }
```

The `Statement` value is a JSON string version of the statement added to the Lambda function policy.

Assigning a Lambda Function to a Campaign

You can assign a Lambda function to an individual Amazon Pinpoint campaign. Or, you can set the Lambda function as the default used by all campaigns for a project, except for those campaigns to which you assign a function individually.

To assign a Lambda function to an individual campaign, use the Amazon Pinpoint API to create or update a http://docs.aws.amazon.com/pinpoint/latest/apireference/rest-api-campaigns.html object, and define its `CampaignHook` attribute. To set a Lambda function as the default for all campaigns in a project, create or update the http://docs.aws.amazon.com/pinpoint/latest/apireference/rest-api-settings.html resource for that project, and define its `CampaignHook` object.

In both cases, set the following `CampaignHook` attributes:

- `LambdaFunctionName` – The name or ARN of the Lambda function that Amazon Pinpoint invokes before sending messages for the campaign.

- `Mode` – Set to `FILTER`. With this mode, Amazon Pinpoint invokes the function and waits for it to return the modified endpoints. After receiving them, Amazon Pinpoint sends the message. Amazon Pinpoint waits for up to 15 seconds before failing the message delivery.

With `CampaignHook` settings defined for a campaign, Amazon Pinpoint invokes the specified Lambda function before sending the campaign's messages. Amazon Pinpoint waits to receive the modified endpoints from the function. If Amazon Pinpoint receives the updated endpoints, it proceeds with the message delivery, using the updated endpoint data.

Creating Campaigns

To help increase engagement between your app and its users, use Amazon Pinpoint to create and manage push notification campaigns that reach out to particular segments of users.

For example, your campaign might invite users back to your app who haven't run it recently or offer special promotions to users who haven't purchased recently.

A campaign sends a tailored message to a user segment that you specify. The campaign can send the message to all users in the segment, or you can allocate a holdout, which is a percentage of users who receive no messages.

You can set the campaign schedule to send the message once or at a recurring frequency, such as once a week. To prevent users from receiving the message at inconvenient times, the schedule can include a quiet time during which no messages are sent.

To experiment with alternative campaign strategies, set up your campaign as an A/B test. An A/B test includes two or more treatments of the message or schedule. Treatments are variations of your message or schedule. As your users respond to the campaign, you can view campaign analytics to compare the effectiveness of each treatment.

For more information, see Campaigns.

Creating Standard Campaigns

A standard campaign sends a custom push notification to a specified segment according to a schedule that you define.

Creating Campaigns With the AWS SDK for Java

The following example demonstrates how to create a campaign with the AWS SDK for Java.

```
1  import com.amazonaws.services.pinpoint.AmazonPinpointClient;
2  import com.amazonaws.services.pinpoint.model.Action;
3  import com.amazonaws.services.pinpoint.model.CampaignResponse;
4  import com.amazonaws.services.pinpoint.model.CreateCampaignRequest;
5  import com.amazonaws.services.pinpoint.model.CreateCampaignResult;
6  import com.amazonaws.services.pinpoint.model.Message;
7  import com.amazonaws.services.pinpoint.model.MessageConfiguration;
8  import com.amazonaws.services.pinpoint.model.Schedule;
9  import com.amazonaws.services.pinpoint.model.WriteCampaignRequest;
10
11 import java.util.ArrayList;
12 import java.util.List;
13
14 public class PinpointCampaignSample {
15
16    public CampaignResponse createCampaign(AmazonPinpointClient client, String appId, String
          segmentId) {
17       Schedule schedule = new Schedule()
18             .withStartTime("IMMEDIATE");
19
20       Message defaultMessage = new Message()
21             .withAction(Action.OPEN_APP)
22             .withBody("My message body.")
23             .withTitle("My message title.");
```

```
24
25        MessageConfiguration messageConfiguration = new MessageConfiguration()
26                .withDefaultMessage(defaultMessage);
27
28        WriteCampaignRequest request = new WriteCampaignRequest()
29                .withDescription("My description.")
30                .withSchedule(schedule)
31                .withSegmentId(segmentId)
32                .withName("MyCampaign")
33                .withMessageConfiguration(messageConfiguration);
34
35        CreateCampaignRequest createCampaignRequest = new CreateCampaignRequest()
36                .withApplicationId(appId).withWriteCampaignRequest(request);
37
38        CreateCampaignResult result = client.createCampaign(createCampaignRequest);
39
40        System.out.println("Campaign ID: " + result.getCampaignResponse().getId());
41
42        return result.getCampaignResponse();
43    }
44
45 }
```

When you run this example, the following is printed to the console window of your IDE:

```
1 Campaign ID: b1c3de717aea4408a75bb3287a906b46
```

Creating A/B Test Campaigns

An A/B test behaves like a standard campaign, but enables you to define different treatments for the campaign message or schedule.

Creating A/B Test Campaigns With the AWS SDK for Java

The following example demonstrates how to create an A/B test campaign with the AWS SDK for Java.

```
1  import com.amazonaws.services.pinpoint.AmazonPinpointClient;
2  import com.amazonaws.services.pinpoint.model.Action;
3  import com.amazonaws.services.pinpoint.model.CampaignResponse;
4  import com.amazonaws.services.pinpoint.model.CreateCampaignRequest;
5  import com.amazonaws.services.pinpoint.model.CreateCampaignResult;
6  import com.amazonaws.services.pinpoint.model.Message;
7  import com.amazonaws.services.pinpoint.model.MessageConfiguration;
8  import com.amazonaws.services.pinpoint.model.Schedule;
9  import com.amazonaws.services.pinpoint.model.WriteCampaignRequest;
10 import com.amazonaws.services.pinpoint.model.WriteTreatmentResource;
11
12 import java.util.ArrayList;
13 import java.util.List;
14
15 public class PinpointCampaignSample {
16
17    public CampaignResponse createAbCampaign(AmazonPinpointClient client, String appId, String
         segmentId) {
```

```
18      Schedule schedule = new Schedule()
19              .withStartTime("IMMEDIATE");
20
21      // Default treatment.
22      Message defaultMessage = new Message()
23              .withAction(Action.OPEN_APP)
24              .withBody("My message body.")
25              .withTitle("My message title.");
26
27      MessageConfiguration messageConfiguration = new MessageConfiguration()
28              .withDefaultMessage(defaultMessage);
29
30      // Additional treatments
31      WriteTreatmentResource treatmentResource = new WriteTreatmentResource()
32              .withMessageConfiguration(messageConfiguration)
33              .withSchedule(schedule)
34              .withSizePercent(40)
35              .withTreatmentDescription("My treatment description.")
36              .withTreatmentName("MyTreatment");
37
38      List<WriteTreatmentResource> additionalTreatments = new ArrayList<WriteTreatmentResource
          >();
39      additionalTreatments.add(treatmentResource);
40
41      WriteCampaignRequest request = new WriteCampaignRequest()
42              .withDescription("My description.")
43              .withSchedule(schedule)
44              .withSegmentId(segmentId)
45              .withName("MyCampaign")
46              .withMessageConfiguration(messageConfiguration)
47              .withAdditionalTreatments(additionalTreatments)
48              .withHoldoutPercent(10); // Hold out of A/B test
49
50      CreateCampaignRequest createCampaignRequest = new CreateCampaignRequest()
51              .withApplicationId(appId).withWriteCampaignRequest(request);
52
53      CreateCampaignResult result = client.createCampaign(createCampaignRequest);
54
55      System.out.println("Campaign ID: " + result.getCampaignResponse().getId());
56
57      return result.getCampaignResponse();
58   }
59
60 }
```

When you run this example, the following is printed to the console window of your IDE:

```
1 Campaign ID: b1c3de717aea4408a75bb3287a906b46
```

Streaming Amazon Pinpoint Events to Kinesis

The Kinesis platform offers services that you can use to load and analyze streaming data on AWS. You can configure Amazon Pinpoint to send events to Amazon Kinesis Data Firehose or Amazon Kinesis Data Streams. By streaming your events, you enable more flexible options for analysis and storage. For more information, and for instructions on how to set up event streaming in the Amazon Pinpoint console, see Streaming App and Campaign Events with Amazon Pinpoint in the *Amazon Pinpoint User Guide*.

Setting up Event Streaming

The following examples demonstrate how to configure Amazon Pinpoint to automatically send the event data from an app to an Kinesis stream or Kinesis Data Firehose delivery stream.

Prerequisites
These examples require the following input:
The app ID of an app that is integrated with Amazon Pinpoint and reporting events. For information about how to integrate, see Integrating Amazon Pinpoint with a Mobile App. The ARN of an Kinesis stream or Kinesis Data Firehose delivery stream in your AWS account. For information about creating these resources, see Amazon Kinesis Data Streams in the *Amazon Kinesis Data Streams Developer Guide* or Creating an Amazon Kinesis Firehose Delivery Stream in the *Amazon Kinesis Firehose Developer Guide*. The ARN of an AWS Identity and Access Management (IAM) role that authorizes Amazon Pinpoint to send data to the stream. For information about creating a role, see IAM Role for Streaming Events to Kinesis.

AWS CLI

The following AWS CLI example uses the http://docs.aws.amazon.com/cli/latest/reference/pinpoint/put-event-stream.html command. This command configures Amazon Pinpoint to send app and campaign events to an Kinesis stream:

```
1 aws pinpoint put-event-stream --application-id application-id --write-event-stream
    DestinationStreamArn=stream-arn,RoleArn=role-arn
```

AWS SDK for Java

The following Java example configures Amazon Pinpoint to send app and campaign events to an Kinesis stream:

```
1  public PutEventStreamResult createEventStream(AmazonPinpoint pinClient, String appId,
2                                                String streamArn, String roleArn) {
3      WriteEventStream stream = new WriteEventStream()
4              .withDestinationStreamArn(streamArn)
5              .withRoleArn(roleArn);
6
7      PutEventStreamRequest request = new PutEventStreamRequest()
8              .withApplicationId(appId)
9              .withWriteEventStream(stream);
10
11     return pinClient.putEventStream(request);
12 }
```

This example constructs a http://docs.aws.amazon.com/AWSJavaSDK/latest/javadoc/com/amazonaws/services/pinpoint/model/WriteEventStream.html object that stores the ARNs of the Kinesis stream and the IAM role. The `WriteEventStream` object is passed to a http://docs.aws.amazon.com/AWSJavaSDK/latest/javadoc/com/amazonaws/services/pinpoint/model/PutEventStreamRequest.html object to configure Amazon

Pinpoint to stream events for a specific app. The `PutEventStreamRequest` object is passed to the http://docs. aws.amazon.com/AWSJavaSDK/latest/javadoc/com/amazonaws/services/pinpoint/AmazonPinpointClient. html#putEventStream-com.amazonaws.services.pinpoint.model.PutEventStreamRequest- method of the Amazon Pinpoint client.

You can assign an Kinesis stream to multiple apps. Amazon Pinpoint will send event data from each app to the stream, enabling you to analyze the data as a collection. The following example method accepts a list of app IDs, and it uses the previous example method, `createEventStream`, to assign a stream to each app:

```
1  public List<PutEventStreamResult> createEventStreamFromAppList(
2         AmazonPinpoint pinClient, List<String> appIDs, String streamArn, String roleArn) {
3     return appIDs.stream()
4             .map(appId -> createEventStream(pinClient, appId, streamArn, roleArn))
5             .collect(Collectors.toList());
6  }
```

With Amazon Pinpoint, you can assign one stream to multiple apps, but you cannot assign multiple streams to one app.

Disabling Event Streaming

If you assigned an Kinesis stream to an app, you can disable event streaming for that app. Amazon Pinpoint stops streaming the events, but you can view analytics based on the events in the Amazon Pinpoint console.

AWS CLI

Use the http://docs.aws.amazon.com/cli/latest/reference/pinpoint/delete-event-stream.html command:

```
1  aws pinpoint delete-event-stream --application-id application-id
```

AWS SDK for Java

Use the http://docs.aws.amazon.com/AWSJavaSDK/latest/javadoc/com/amazonaws/services/ pinpoint/AmazonPinpointClient.html#deleteEventStream-com.amazonaws.services.pinpoint.model. DeleteEventStreamRequest- method of the Amazon Pinpoint client:

```
1  pinClient.deleteEventStream(new DeleteEventStreamRequest().withApplicationId(appId));
```

Event Data

After you set up event streaming, Amazon Pinpoint sends each event reported by your application, and each campaign event created by Amazon Pinpoint, as a JSON data object to your Kinesis stream.

The event type is indicated by the `event_type` attribute in the event JSON object.

App Events

After you integrate your app with Amazon Pinpoint and you run one or more campaigns, Amazon Pinpoint streams events about user activity and campaign message deliveries.

Example

The JSON object for an app event contains the data shown in the following example.

```json
{
  "event_type": "_session.stop",
  "event_timestamp": 1487973802507,
  "arrival_timestamp": 1487973803515,
  "event_version": "3.0",
  "application": {
    "app_id": "a1b2c3d4e5f6g7h8i9j0k1l2m3n4o5p6",
    "cognito_identity_pool_id": "us-east-1:a1b2c3d4-e5f6-g7h8-i9j0-k1l2m3n4o5p6",
    "package_name": "main.page",
    "sdk": {
      "name": "aws-sdk-mobile-analytics-js",
      "version": "0.9.1:2.4.8"
    },
    "title": "title",
    "version_name": "1.0",
    "version_code": "1"
  },
  "client": {
    "client_id": "m3n4o5p6-a1b2-c3d4-e5f6-g7h8i9j0k1l2",
    "cognito_id": "us-east-1:i9j0k1l2-m3n4-o5p6-a1b2-c3d4e5f6g7h8"
  },
  "device": {
    "locale": {
      "code": "en_US",
      "country": "US",
      "language": "en"
    },
    "make": "generic web browser",
    "model": "Unknown",
    "platform": {
      "name": "android",
      "version": "10.10"
    }
  },
  "session": {
    "session_id": "f549dea9-1090-945d-c3d1-e496780baac5",
    "start_timestamp": 1487973202531,
    "stop_timestamp": 1487973802507
  },
  "attributes": {},
  "metrics": {}
}
```

Standard App Event Types

Amazon Pinpoint streams the following standard types for app events:

- _campaign.send
- _monetization.purchase
- _session.start

- _session.stop

- _session.pause

- _session.resume

- _userauth.sign_in

- _userauth.sign_up

- _userauth.auth_fail

Email Events

If the email channel is enabled, Amazon Pinpoint streams events about email deliveries, complaints, opens, and more.

Example

The JSON object for an email event contains the data shown in the following example.

```
1  {
2    "event_type": "_email.delivered",
3    "event_timestamp": 1487973802507,
4    "arrival_timestamp": 1487973803515,
5    "event_version": "3.0",
6    "application": {
7      "app_id": "a1b2c3d4e5f6g7h8i9j0k1l2m3n4o5p6",
8      "cognito_identity_pool_id": "us-east-1:a1b2c3d4-e5f6-g7h8-i9j0-k1l2m3n4o5p6",
9      "package_name": "main.page",
10     "sdk": {
11       "name": "aws-sdk-mobile-analytics-js",
12       "version": "0.9.1:2.4.8"
13     },
14     "title": "title",
15     "version_name": "1.0",
16     "version_code": "1"
17   },
18   "client": {
19     "client_id": "m3n4o5p6-a1b2-c3d4-e5f6-g7h8i9j0k1l2",
20     "cognito_id": "us-east-1:i9j0k1l2-m3n4-o5p6-a1b2-c3d4e5f6g7h8"
21   },
22   "device": {
23     "locale": {
24       "code": "en_US",
25       "country": "US",
26       "language": "en"
27     },
28     "make": "generic web browser",
29     "model": "Unknown",
30     "platform": {
31       "name": "android",
32       "version": "10.10"
33     }
34   },
35   "session": {
36     "session_id": "f549dea9-1090-945d-c3d1-e496780baac5",
```

```
37      "start_timestamp": 1487973202531,
38      "stop_timestamp": 1487973802507
39    },
40    "attributes": {},
41    "metrics": {}
42 }
```

Standard Email Event Types

Amazon Pinpoint streams the following standard types for the email channel:

- _email.send
- _email.delivered
- _email.rejected
- _email.hardbounce
- _email.softbounce
- _email.complaint
- _email.open
- _email.click
- _email.unsubscribe

SMS Events

If the SMS channel is enabled, Amazon Pinpoint streams events about SMS deliveries.

Example

The JSON object for an SMS event contains the data shown in the following example.

```
1  {
2    "account_id": "123412341234",
3    "event_type": "_SMS.SUCCESS",
4    "arrival_timestamp": 2345678,
5    "timestamp": 13425345,
6    "timestamp_created": "1495756908285",
7    "application_key": "AppKey-688037015201",
8    "unique_id": "uniqueId-688037015201140879759 69",
9    "attributes": {
10     "message_id": "12234sdv",
11     "sender_request_id": "abdfg",
12     "number_of_message_parts": 1,
13     "record_status": "SUCCESS",
14     "message_type": "Transactional",
15     "keyword": "test",
16     "mcc_mnc": "456123",
17     "iso_country_code": "US"
18   },
19   "metrics": {
20     "price_in_millicents_usd": 0.0
21   },
```

```
22    "facets": {},
23    "additional_properties": {}
24 }
```

Standard SMS Event Types

Amazon Pinpoint streams the following standard types for the SMS channel:

- _sms.send

- _sms.success

- _sms.fail

- _sms.optout

Event Attributes

The JSON object for an event contains the following attributes.

Event

Attribute	Description
event_type	The type of event reported by your app.
event_timestamp	The time at which the event is reported as Unix time in milliseconds. If your app reports events using the AWS Mobile SDK for Android or the AWS Mobile SDK for iOS, the time stamp is automatically generated.
arrival_timestamp	The time at which the event is received by Amazon Pinpoint as Unix time in milliseconds. Does not apply to campaign events.
event_version	The version of the event JSON schema.Check this version in your event-processing application so that you know when to update the application in response to a schema update.
application	Your Amazon Pinpoint app. See the Application table.
client	The app client installed on the device that reports the event. See the Client table.
device	The device that reports the event. See the Device table.
session	The app session on the device. Typically a session begins when a user opens your app.
attributes	Custom attributes that your app reports to Amazon Pinpoint as part of the event.
metrics	Custom metrics that your app reports to Amazon Pinpoint as part of the event.

Application

Attribute	Description
app_id	The unique ID of the Amazon Pinpoint app that reports the event.

Attribute	Description
cognito_identity_pool_id	The unique ID of the Amazon Cognito identity pool used by your app.
package_name	The name of your app package. For example, com.example.my_app.
sdk	The SDK used to report the event.
title	The title of your app.
version_name	The customer-facing app version, such as V2.0.
version_code	The internal code that represents your app version.

Client

Attribute	Description
client_id	The unique ID for the app client installed on the device. This ID is automatically generated by the AWS Mobile SDK for iOS and the AWS Mobile SDK for Android.
cognito_id	The unique ID assigned to the app client in the Amazon Cognito identity pool used by your app.

Device

Attribute	Description
locale	The device locale.
make	The device make, such as Apple or Samsung.
model	The device model, such as iPhone.
platform	The device platform, such as ios or android.

Session

Attribute	Description
session_id	The unique ID for the app session.
start_timestamp	The time at which the session starts as Unix time in milliseconds.
stop_timestamp	The time at which the session stops as Unix time in milliseconds.

Logging Amazon Pinpoint API Calls with AWS CloudTrail

Amazon Pinpoint is integrated with AWS CloudTrail, a service that provides a record of actions taken by a user, role, or an AWS service in Amazon Pinpoint. If you create a trail, you can enable continuous delivery of CloudTrail events to an Amazon S3 bucket, Amazon CloudWatch Logs, and Amazon CloudWatch Events. Using the information collected by CloudTrail, you can determine the request that was made to Amazon Pinpoint, the IP address the request was made from, who made the request, when it was made, and additional details.

To learn more about CloudTrail, including how to configure and enable it, see the AWS CloudTrail User Guide.

Amazon Pinpoint Information in CloudTrail

Amazon Pinpoint supports logging the following actions as events in CloudTrail log files:

- CreateApp
- CreateCampaign
- CreateImportJob
- CreateSegment
- DeleteAdmChannel
- DeleteApnsChannel
- DeleteApnsSandboxChannel
- DeleteApnsVoipChannel
- DeleteApnsVoipSandboxChannel
- DeleteApp
- DeleteBaiduChannel
- DeleteCampaign
- DeleteEmailChannel
- DeleteEventStream
- DeleteGcmChannel
- DeleteSegment
- DeleteSmsChannel
- GetAdmChannel
- GetApnsChannel
- GetApnsSandboxChannel
- GetApnsVoipChannel
- GetApnsVoipSandboxChannel
- GetApp
- GetApplicationSettings
- GetApps
- GetBaiduChannel
- GetCampaign

- GetCampaignActivities

- GetCampaignVersion

- GetCampaignVersions

- GetCampaigns

- GetEmailChannel

- GetEventStream

- GetGcmChannel

- GetImportJob

- GetImportJobs

- GetSegment

- GetSegmentImportJobs

- GetSegmentVersion

- GetSegmentVersions

- GetSegments

- GetSmsChannel

- PutEventStream

- UpdateAdmChannel

- UpdateApnsChannel

- UpdateApnsSandboxChannel

- UpdateApnsVoipChannel

- UpdateApnsVoipSandboxChannel

- UpdateApplicationSettings

- UpdateBaiduChannel

- UpdateCampaign

- UpdateEmailChannel

- UpdateGcmChannel

- UpdateSegment

- UpdateSmsChannel

Important
The following Amazon Pinpoint actions are not logged in CloudTrail:
GetEndpoint SendMessages SendUsersMessages UpdateEndpoint UpdateEndpointsBatch

Every event or log entry contains information about who generated the request. The identity information helps you determine the following:

- Whether the request was made with root or IAM user credentials.

- Whether the request was made with temporary security credentials for a role or federated user.

- Whether the request was made by another AWS service.

For more information, see the CloudTrail userIdentity Element.

You can create a trail and store your log files in your Amazon S3 bucket for as long as you want, and define Amazon S3 lifecycle rules to archive or delete log files automatically. By default, your log files are encrypted with Amazon S3 server-side encryption (SSE).

To be notified of log file delivery, configure CloudTrail to publish Amazon SNS notifications when new log files are delivered. For more information, see Configuring Amazon SNS Notifications for CloudTrail.

You can also aggregate Amazon Pinpoint log files from multiple AWS Regions and multiple AWS accounts into a single Amazon S3 bucket.

For more information, see Receiving CloudTrail Log Files from Multiple Regions and Receiving CloudTrail Log Files from Multiple Accounts.

Example: Amazon Pinpoint Log File Entries

A trail is a configuration that enables delivery of events as log files to an Amazon S3 bucket that you specify. CloudTrail log files contain one or more log entries. An event represents a single request from any source and includes information about the requested action, the date and time of the action, request parameters, and so on. CloudTrail log files are not an ordered stack trace of the public API calls, so they do not appear in any specific order.

The following example shows a CloudTrail log entry that demonstrates the `GetCampaigns` and `CreateCampaign` actions.

```
 1  {
 2    "Records": [
 3      {
 4        "awsRegion": "us-east-1",
 5        "eventID": "example0-09a3-47d6-a810-c5f9fd2534fe",
 6        "eventName": "GetCampaigns",
 7        "eventSource": "pinpoint.amazonaws.com",
 8        "eventTime": "2018-02-03T00:56:48Z",
 9        "eventType": "AwsApiCall",
10        "eventVersion": "1.05",
11        "readOnly": true,
12        "recipientAccountId": "123456789012",
13        "requestID": "example1-b9bb-50fa-abdb-80f274981d60",
14        "requestParameters": {
15          "application-id": "example71dfa4c1aab66332a5839798f",
16          "page-size": "1000"
17        },
18        "responseElements": null,
19        "sourceIPAddress": "192.0.2.0",
20        "userAgent": "Jersey/${project.version} (HttpUrlConnection 1.8.0_144)",
21        "userIdentity": {
22          "accessKeyId": "AKIAIOSFODNN7EXAMPLE",
23          "accountId": "123456789012",
24          "arn": "arn:aws:iam::123456789012:root",
25          "principalId": "123456789012",
26          "sessionContext": {
27            "attributes": {
28              "creationDate": "2018-02-02T16:55:29Z",
29              "mfaAuthenticated": "false"
30            }
31          },
```

```
32        "type": "Root"
33      }
34    },
35    {
36      "awsRegion": "us-east-1",
37      "eventID": "example0-09a3-47d6-a810-c5f9fd2534fe",
38      "eventName": "CreateCampaign",
39      "eventSource": "pinpoint.amazonaws.com",
40      "eventTime": "2018-02-03T01:05:16Z",
41      "eventType": "AwsApiCall",
42      "eventVersion": "1.05",
43      "readOnly": false,
44      "recipientAccountId": "123456789012",
45      "requestID": "example1-b9bb-50fa-abdb-80f274981d60",
46      "requestParameters": {
47        "Description": "***",
48        "HoldoutPercent": 0,
49        "IsPaused": false,
50        "MessageConfiguration": "***",
51        "Name": "***",
52        "Schedule": {
53          "Frequency": "ONCE",
54          "IsLocalTime": true,
55          "StartTime": "2018-02-03T00:00:00-08:00",
56          "Timezone": "utc-08"
57        },
58        "SegmentId": "exampleda204adf991a80281aa0e591",
59        "SegmentVersion": 1,
60        "application-id": "example71dfa4c1aab66332a5839798f"
61      },
62      "responseElements": {
63        "ApplicationId": "example71dfa4c1aab66332a5839798f",
64        "CreationDate": "2018-02-03T01:05:16.425Z",
65        "Description": "***",
66        "HoldoutPercent": 0,
67        "Id": "example54a654f80948680cbba240ede",
68        "IsPaused": false,
69        "LastModifiedDate": "2018-02-03T01:05:16.425Z",
70        "MessageConfiguration": "***",
71        "Name": "***",
72        "Schedule": {
73          "Frequency": "ONCE",
74          "IsLocalTime": true,
75          "StartTime": "2018-02-03T00:00:00-08:00",
76          "Timezone": "utc-08"
77        },
78        "SegmentId": "example4da204adf991a80281example",
79        "SegmentVersion": 1,
80        "State": {
81          "CampaignStatus": "SCHEDULED"
82        },
83        "Version": 1
84      },
85      "sourceIPAddress": "192.0.2.0",
```

102

```
86      "userAgent": "aws-cli/1.14.9 Python/3.4.3 Linux/3.4.0+ botocore/1.8.34",
87      "userIdentity": {
88        "accessKeyId": "AKIAIOSFODNN7EXAMPLE",
89        "accountId": "123456789012",
90        "arn": "arn:aws:iam::123456789012:user/userName",
91        "principalId": "AIDAIHTHRCDA62EXAMPLE",
92        "type": "IAMUser",
93        "userName": "userName"
94      }
95    }
96  ]
97 }
```

Permissions

To use Amazon Pinpoint, users in your AWS account require permissions that allow them to view analytics data, define user segments, create and deploy campaigns, and more. Users of your app also require access to Amazon Pinpoint so that your app can register endpoints and report usage data. To grant access to Amazon Pinpoint features, create AWS Identity and Access Management (IAM) policies that allow Amazon Pinpoint actions.

IAM is a service that helps you securely control access to AWS resources. IAM policies include statements that allow or deny specific actions that users can perform on specific resources. Amazon Pinpoint provides a set of actions for IAM policies that you can use to specify granular permissions for Amazon Pinpoint users. You can grant the appropriate level of access to Amazon Pinpoint without creating overly permissive policies that might expose important data or compromise your campaigns. For example, you can grant unrestricted access to an Amazon Pinpoint administrator, and grant read-only access to individuals in your organization who only need access to analytics.

For more information about IAM policies, see Overview of IAM Policies in the *IAM User Guide*.

When you add your app to Amazon Pinpoint by creating a project in AWS Mobile Hub, Mobile Hub automatically provisions AWS resources for app user authentication. Mobile Hub creates an Amazon Cognito identity pool so that app users can authenticate with AWS. Mobile Hub also creates an IAM role that allows app users to register with Amazon Pinpoint and report usage data. You can customize these resources as needed for your app.

To import endpoint definitions, you must grant Amazon Pinpoint read-only access to an Amazon S3 bucket.

- IAM Policies for Amazon Pinpoint Users
- User Authentication in Amazon Pinpoint Apps
- AWS Mobile Hub Service Role
- IAM Role for Importing Segments
- IAM Role for Streaming Events to Kinesis

IAM Policies for Amazon Pinpoint Users

You can add Amazon Pinpoint API actions to AWS Identity and Access Management (IAM) policies to allow or deny specific actions for Amazon Pinpoint users in your account. The Amazon Pinpoint API actions in your policies control what users can do in the Amazon Pinpoint console. These actions also control which programmatic requests users can make with the AWS SDKs, the AWS CLI, or the Amazon Pinpoint REST API.

In a policy, you specify each action with the `mobiletargeting` namespace followed by a colon and the name of the action, such as `GetSegments`. Most actions correspond to a request to the Amazon Pinpoint REST API using a specific URI and HTTP method. For example, if you allow the `mobiletargeting:GetSegments` action in a user's policy, the user is allowed to make an HTTP GET request against the http://docs.aws.amazon.com/pinpoint/latest/apireference/rest-api-segments.html#rest-api-segments-list URI. This policy also allows the user to view the segments for an app in the console, and to retrieve the segments by using an AWS SDK or the AWS CLI.

Each action is performed on a specific Amazon Pinpoint resource, which you identify in a policy statement by its Amazon Resource Name (ARN). For example, the `mobiletargeting:GetSegments` action is performed on a specific app, which you identify with the ARN, `arn:aws:mobiletargeting:region:account-id:/apps/application-id`.

You can refer generically to all Amazon Pinpoint actions or resources by using wildcards ("*"). For example, to allow all actions for all resources, include the following in a policy statement:

```
1 "Effect": "Allow",
2 "Action": "mobiletargeting:*",
3 "Resource": "*"
```

Example Policies

The following examples demonstrate how you can manage Amazon Pinpoint access with IAM policies.

Amazon Pinpoint Administrator

The following administrator policy allows full access to Amazon Pinpoint actions and resources:

```
1  {
2      "Version": "2012-10-17",
3      "Statement": [
4          {
5              "Effect": "Allow",
6              "Action": [
7                  "mobiletargeting:*",
8                  "mobileanalytics:*"
9              ],
10             "Resource": "*"
11         }
12     ]
13 }
```

In addition to the Amazon Pinpoint actions, this policy allows all Amazon Mobile Analytics actions with `mobileanalytics:*`. Amazon Pinpoint and Amazon Mobile Analytics share data about your apps, so you must include permissions for both services in policies for Amazon Pinpoint users.

Read-Only Access

The following policy allows read-only access for all apps in an account:

```
1  {
2    "Version": "2012-10-17",
3    "Statement": [
4      {
5        "Action": [
6          "mobiletargeting:GetEndpoint",
7          "mobiletargeting:GetSegment*",
8          "mobiletargeting:GetCampaign*",
9          "mobiletargeting:GetImport*",
10         "mobiletargeting:GetApnsChannel",
11         "mobiletargeting:GetGcmChannel",
12         "mobiletargeting:GetApplicationSettings",
13         "mobiletargeting:GetEventStream"
14       ],
15       "Effect": "Allow",
16       "Resource": "arn:aws:mobiletargeting:*:account-id:apps/*"
17     },
18     {
19       "Action": "mobiletargeting:GetReports",
20       "Effect": "Allow",
21       "Resource": "arn:aws:mobiletargeting:*:account-id:reports"
22     },
23     {
24       "Action": "mobileanalytics:ListApps",
25       "Effect": "Allow",
26       "Resource": "*"
27     }
28   ]
29 }
```

API Actions for IAM Policies

You can add the following API actions to IAM policies to manage what Amazon Pinpoint users in your account are allowed to do.

mobiletargeting:GetEndpoint
Retrieve information about a specific endpoint.

- URI – http://docs.aws.amazon.com/pinpoint/latest/apireference/rest-api-endpoints.html#rest-api-endpoints-instance

- Method – GET

- Resource ARN – `arn:aws:mobiletargeting:region:account-id:apps/application-id/endpoints/endpoint-id`

mobiletargeting:UpdateEndpoint
Create an endpoint or update the information for an endpoint.

- URI – http://docs.aws.amazon.com/pinpoint/latest/apireference/rest-api-endpoints.html#rest-api-endpoints-instance

- Method – PUT

- Resource ARN – `arn:aws:mobiletargeting:region:account-id:apps/application-id/endpoints/endpoint-id`

`mobiletargeting:UpdateEndpointsBatch`
Create or update endpoints as a batch operation.

- URI – http://docs.aws.amazon.com/pinpoint/latest/apireference/rest-api-endpoints.html#rest-api-endpoints-list

- Method – PUT

- Resource ARN – `arn:aws:mobiletargeting:region:account-id:apps/application-id`

`mobiletargeting:CreateSegment`
Create a segment that is based on endpoint data reported to Amazon Pinpoint by your app. To allow a user to create a segment by importing endpoint data from outside of Amazon Pinpoint, allow the `mobiletargeting:CreateImportJob` action.

- URI – http://docs.aws.amazon.com/pinpoint/latest/apireference/rest-api-segments.html#rest-api-segments-list

- Method – POST

- Resource ARN – `arn:aws:mobiletargeting:region:account-id:apps/application-id`

`mobiletargeting:DeleteSegment`
Delete a specific segment.

- URI – http://docs.aws.amazon.com/pinpoint/latest/apireference/rest-api-segments.html#rest-api-segments-instance

- Method – DELETE

- Resource ARN – `arn:aws:mobiletargeting:region:account-id:apps/application-id/segments/segment-id`

`mobiletargeting:GetSegment`
Retrieve information about a specific segment.

- URI – http://docs.aws.amazon.com/pinpoint/latest/apireference/rest-api-segments.html#rest-api-segments-instance

- Method – GET

- Resource ARN – `arn:aws:mobiletargeting:region:account-id:apps/application-id/segments/segment-id`

`mobiletargeting:GetSegments`
Retrieve information about the segments for an app.

- URI – http://docs.aws.amazon.com/pinpoint/latest/apireference/rest-api-segments.html#rest-api-segments-list

- Method – GET

- Resource ARN – `arn:aws:mobiletargeting:region:account-id:apps/application-id`

`mobiletargeting:GetSegmentImportJobs`
Retrieve information about jobs that create segments by importing endpoint definitions from Amazon S3.

- URI – http://docs.aws.amazon.com/pinpoint/latest/apireference/rest-api-jobs-import.html#rest-api-jobs-import-list-segment

- Method – GET

- Resource ARN – `arn:aws:mobiletargeting:region:account-id:apps/application-id/segments/segment-id`

`mobiletargeting:GetSegmentVersion`
Retrieve information about a specific segment version.

- URI – http://docs.aws.amazon.com/pinpoint/latest/apireference/rest-api-segments.html#rest-api-segments-version-instance

- Method – GET

- Resource ARN – `arn:aws:mobiletargeting:region:account-id:apps/application-id/segments/segment-id`

`mobiletargeting:GetSegmentVersions`
Retrieve information about the current and prior versions of a segment.

- URI – http://docs.aws.amazon.com/pinpoint/latest/apireference/rest-api-segments.html#rest-api-segments-versions-list

- Method – GET

- Resource ARN – `arn:aws:mobiletargeting:region:account-id:apps/application-id/segments/segment-id`

`mobiletargeting:UpdateSegment`
Update a specific segment.

- URI – http://docs.aws.amazon.com/pinpoint/latest/apireference/rest-api-segments.html#rest-api-segments-instance

- Method – PUT

- Resource ARN – `arn:aws:mobiletargeting:region:account-id:apps/application-id/segments/segment-id`

`mobiletargeting:CreateCampaign`
Create a campaign for an app.

- URI – http://docs.aws.amazon.com/pinpoint/latest/apireference/rest-api-campaigns.html#rest-api-campaigns-list

- Method – POST

- Resource ARN – `arn:aws:mobiletargeting:region:account-id:apps/application-id`

`mobiletargeting:DeleteCampaign`
Delete a specific campaign.

- URI – http://docs.aws.amazon.com/pinpoint/latest/apireference/rest-api-campaigns.html#rest-api-campaigns-instance

- Method – DELETE

- Resource ARN – `arn:aws:mobiletargeting:region:account-id:/apps/application-id/campaigns/campaign-id`

`mobiletargeting:GetCampaign`
Retrieve information about a specific campaign.

- URI – http://docs.aws.amazon.com/pinpoint/latest/apireference/rest-api-campaigns.html#rest-api-campaigns-instance

- Method – GET

- Resource ARN – `arn:aws:mobiletargeting:region:account-id:apps/application-id/campaigns/campaign-id`

`mobiletargeting:GetCampaignActivities`
Retrieve information about the activities performed by a campaign.

- URI – http://docs.aws.amazon.com/pinpoint/latest/apireference/rest-api-activities.html#rest-api-activities-list
- Method – GET
- Resource ARN – `arn:aws:mobiletargeting:region:account-id:apps/application-id/campaigns/campaign-id`

`mobiletargeting:GetCampaigns`
Retrieve information about all campaigns for an app.

- URI – http://docs.aws.amazon.com/pinpoint/latest/apireference/rest-api-campaigns.html#rest-api-campaigns-list
- Method – GET
- Resource ARN – `arn:aws:mobiletargeting:region:account-id:apps/application-id`

`mobiletargeting:GetCampaignVersion`
Retrieve information about a specific campaign version.

- URI – http://docs.aws.amazon.com/pinpoint/latest/apireference/rest-api-campaigns.html#rest-api-campaigns-version-instance
- Method – GET
- Resource ARN – `arn:aws:mobiletargeting:region:account-id:apps/application-id/campaigns/campaign-id`

`mobiletargeting:GetCampaignVersions`
Retrieve information about the current and prior versions of a campaign.

- URI – http://docs.aws.amazon.com/pinpoint/latest/apireference/rest-api-campaigns.html#rest-api-campaigns-versions-list
- Method – GET
- Resource ARN – `arn:aws:mobiletargeting:region:account-id:apps/application-id/campaigns/campaign-id`

`mobiletargeting:UpdateCampaign`
Update a specific campaign.

- URI – http://docs.aws.amazon.com/pinpoint/latest/apireference/rest-api-campaigns.html#rest-api-campaigns-instance
- Method – PUT
- Resource ARN – `arn:aws:mobiletargeting:region:account-id:apps/application-id/campaigns/campaign-id`

`mobiletargeting:CreateImportJob`
Import endpoint definitions from Amazon S3 to create a segment.

- URI – http://docs.aws.amazon.com/pinpoint/latest/apireference/rest-api-jobs-import.html#rest-api-jobs-import-list
- Method – POST
- Resource ARN – `arn:aws:mobiletargeting:region:account-id:apps/application-id`

`mobiletargeting:GetImportJob`

Retrieve information about a specific import job.

- URI – http://docs.aws.amazon.com/pinpoint/latest/apireference/rest-api-jobs-import.html#rest-api-jobs-import-instance

- Method – GET

- Resource ARN – `arn:aws:mobiletargeting:region:account-id:apps/application-id/jobs/import/job-id`

`mobiletargeting:GetImportJobs`

Retrieve information about all import jobs for an app.

- URI – http://docs.aws.amazon.com/pinpoint/latest/apireference/rest-api-jobs-import.html#rest-api-jobs-import-list

- Method – GET

- Resource ARN – `arn:aws:mobiletargeting:region:account-id:apps/application-id`

`mobiletargeting:DeleteApnsChannel`

Delete the APNs channel for an app.

- URI – http://docs.aws.amazon.com/pinpoint/latest/apireference/rest-api-channels-apns.html#rest-api-channels-apns

- Method – DELETE

- Resource ARN – `arn:aws:mobiletargeting:region:account-id:apps/application-id/channels/apns`

`mobiletargeting:GetApnsChannel`

Retrieve information about the APNs channel for an app.

- URI – http://docs.aws.amazon.com/pinpoint/latest/apireference/rest-api-channels-apns.html#rest-api-channels-apns

- Method – GET

- Resource ARN – `arn:aws:mobiletargeting:region:account-id:apps/application-id/channels/apns`

`mobiletargeting:UpdateApnsChannel`

Update the Apple Push Notification service (APNs) certificate and private key, which allow Amazon Pinpoint to send push notifications to your iOS app.

- URI – http://docs.aws.amazon.com/pinpoint/latest/apireference/rest-api-channels-apns.html#rest-api-channels-apns

- Method – PUT

- Resource ARN – `arn:aws:mobiletargeting:region:account-id:apps/application-id/channels/apns`

`mobiletargeting:DeleteGcmChannel`

Delete the GCM channel for an app.

- URI – http://docs.aws.amazon.com/pinpoint/latest/apireference/rest-api-channels-gcm.html#rest-api-channels-gcm

- Method – DELETE

- Resource ARN – `arn:aws:mobiletargeting:region:account-id:apps/application-id/channels/gcm`

`mobiletargeting:GetGcmChannel`
Retrieve information about the GCM channel for an app.

- URI – http://docs.aws.amazon.com/pinpoint/latest/apireference/rest-api-channels-gcm.html#rest-api-channels-gcm

- Method – GET

- Resource ARN – `arn:aws:mobiletargeting:region:account-id:apps/application-id/channels/gcm`

`mobiletargeting:UpdateGcmChannel`
Update the Firebase Cloud Messaging (FCM) or Google Cloud Messaging (GCM) API key, which allows Amazon Pinpoint to send push notifications to your Android app.

- URI – http://docs.aws.amazon.com/pinpoint/latest/apireference/rest-api-channels-gcm.html#rest-api-channels-gcm

- Method – PUT

- Resource ARN – `arn:aws:mobiletargeting:region:account-id:apps/application-id/channels/gcm`

`mobiletargeting:GetApplicationSettings`
Retrieve the default settings for an app.

- URI – http://docs.aws.amazon.com/pinpoint/latest/apireference/rest-api-settings.html#rest-api-settings

- Method – GET

- Resource ARN – `arn:aws:mobiletargeting:region:account-id:apps/application-id`

`mobiletargeting:UpdateApplicationSettings`
Update the default settings for an app.

- URI – http://docs.aws.amazon.com/pinpoint/latest/apireference/rest-api-settings.html#rest-api-settings

- Method – PUT

- Resource ARN – `arn:aws:mobiletargeting:region:account-id:apps/application-id`

`mobiletargeting:DeleteEventStream`
Delete the event stream for an app.

- URI – http://docs.aws.amazon.com/pinpoint/latest/apireference/rest-api-eventstreams.html#rest-api-eventstream-instance

- Method – DELETE

- Resource ARN – `arn:aws:mobiletargeting:region:account-id:apps/application-id/eventstream`

`mobiletargeting:GetEventStream`
Retrieve information about the event stream for an app.

- URI – http://docs.aws.amazon.com/pinpoint/latest/apireference/rest-api-eventstreams.html#rest-api-eventstream-instance

- Method – GET

- Resource ARN – `arn:aws:mobiletargeting:region:account-id:apps/application-id/eventstream`

`mobiletargeting:PutEventStream`
Create or update an event stream for an app.

- URI – http://docs.aws.amazon.com/pinpoint/latest/apireference/rest-api-eventstreams.html#rest-api-eventstream-instance

- Method – PUT

- Resource ARN – `arn:aws:mobiletargeting:region:account-id:apps/application-id/eventstream`

`mobiletargeting:GetReports`

View analytics in the Amazon Pinpoint console.

- URI – Not applicable

- Method – Not applicable

- Resource ARN – `arn:aws:mobiletargeting:region:account-id:reports`

User Authentication in Amazon Pinpoint Apps

To integrate with Amazon Pinpoint, your app must authenticate users to register endpoints and report usage data. When you add your app to Amazon Pinpoint by creating a project in AWS Mobile Hub, Mobile Hub automatically provisions the following AWS resources to help you implement user authentication:

Amazon Cognito identity pool
Amazon Cognito creates unique identities for your users and provides credentials that grant temporary access to the backend AWS resources for your app. An identity pool is a store of user identity data for your app users. Amazon Cognito provides credentials for authenticated and unauthenticated users. Authenticated users include those who sign in to your app through a public identity provider, such as Facebook, Amazon, or Google. Unauthenticated users are those who do not sign in to your app, such as guest users.
You control your users' access to AWS resources with separate AWS Identity and Access Management (IAM) roles for authenticated and unauthenticated users. These roles must be assigned to the identity pool.

IAM role for unauthenticated users
Includes permissions policies that delegate limited access to AWS resources for unauthenticated users. You can customize the role as needed. By default, this role is assigned to the Amazon Cognito identity pool.

If your app requires users to authenticate with a public identity provider, you must create an IAM role for authenticated users and assign this role to the identity pool. To support Amazon Pinpoint, the permissions in your authenticated role must include the same permissions as those in the unauthenticated role created by Mobile Hub.

For more information about IAM roles, see IAM Roles in the *IAM User Guide*.

Your app code uses Amazon Cognito and IAM to authenticate users as follows:

1. Your app code constructs an Amazon Cognito credentials provider.

2. Your app code passes the provider as a parameter when it initializes the Amazon Pinpoint client.

3. The Amazon Pinpoint client uses the provider to get credentials for the user's identity in the identity pool. New users are assigned a new identity.

4. The user gains the permissions granted by the IAM roles that are associated with the identity pool.

For code examples that show how to construct the credentials provider and initialize the Amazon Pinpoint client, see Initializing the Amazon Pinpoint Client (iOS) and Initializing the Amazon Pinpoint Client (Android).

For more information about how Amazon Cognito supports user authentication, see Amazon Cognito Identity: Using Federated Identities in the *Amazon Cognito Developer Guide*.

Unauthenticated Role

The unauthenticated role created by Mobile Hub allows your app users to send data to Amazon Pinpoint. The role name includes "unauth_MOBILEHUB"; for example, in the IAM console, you will see a role with a name similar to MySampleApp_unauth_MOBILEHUB_1234567890.

IAM roles delegate permissions with two types of policies:

- Permissions policy – Grants the user of the role permission to take the specified actions on the specified resources.

- Trust policy – Specifies which entities are allowed to assume the role and gain its permissions.

Permissions Policies

The unauthenticated role includes two permissions policies. The following permissions policy allows your app users to register with Amazon Pinpoint and report app usage events. Mobile Hub assigns the policy a name that includes "`mobileanalytics_MOBILEHUB`".

```
 1  {
 2    "Version": "2012-10-17",
 3    "Statement": [
 4      {
 5        "Effect": "Allow",
 6        "Action": [
 7          "mobileanalytics:PutEvents"
 8        ],
 9        "Resource": [
10          "*"
11        ]
12      },
13      {
14        "Effect": "Allow",
15        "Action": [
16          "mobiletargeting:UpdateEndpoint"
17        ],
18        "Resource": [
19          "arn:aws:mobiletargeting:*:*:apps/*"
20        ]
21      }
22    ]
23  }
```

After your app is integrated with Amazon Pinpoint, your app registers an endpoint with Amazon Pinpoint when a new user starts an app session. Your app sends updated endpoint data to Amazon Pinpoint each time the user starts a new session.

The following permissions policy allows your app users to establish an identity with the Amazon Cognito identity pool for your app. Mobile Hub assigns the policy a name that includes "`signin_MOBILEHUB`".

```
 1  {
 2    "Version": "2012-10-17",
 3    "Statement": [
 4      {
 5        "Effect": "Allow",
 6        "Action": [
 7          "cognito-identity:GetId"
 8        ],
 9        "Resource": [
10          "arn:aws:cognito-identity:*:*:identityPool/us-east-1:1a2b3c4d-5e6f-7g8h-9i0j-1
               k2l3m4n5o6p"
11        ]
12      }
13    ]
14  }
```

Trust Policy

To allow Amazon Cognito to assume the role for unauthenticated users in your identity pool, Mobile Hub adds the following trust policy to the role:

```
1  {
2    "Version": "2012-10-17",
3    "Statement": [
4      {
5        "Sid": "",
6        "Effect": "Allow",
7        "Principal": {
8          "Federated": "cognito-identity.amazonaws.com"
9        },
10       "Action": "sts:AssumeRoleWithWebIdentity",
11       "Condition": {
12         "StringEquals": {
13           "cognito-identity.amazonaws.com:aud": "us-east-1:1a2b3c4d-5e6f-7g8h-9i0j-1k2l3m4n5o6p"
14         },
15         "ForAnyValue:StringLike": {
16           "cognito-identity.amazonaws.com:amr": "unauthenticated"
17         }
18       }
19     }
20   ]
21 }
```

For an example of a trust policy assigned to an authenticated role, see Role-Based Access Control in the *Amazon Cognito Developer Guide*.

AWS Mobile Hub Service Role

AWS Mobile Hub creates an AWS Identity and Access Management (IAM) role in your AWS account when you agree to a one-time request in the Mobile Hub console to manage AWS resources and services for you. This role, called `MobileHub_Service_Role`, allows Mobile Hub to create and modify your AWS resources and services for your Mobile Hub project.

For more information about the Mobile Hub service role, see Mobile Hub Service Role and Policies Used on Your Behalf in the *AWS Mobile Hub Developer Guide*.

To add an app to Amazon Pinpoint, you create a Mobile Hub project and configure it to include the User Engagement feature. To support this feature, Mobile Hub adds the following permissions to the Mobile Hub service role:

```
1  {
2    "Effect": "Allow",
3    "Action": [
4      "mobiletargeting:UpdateApnsChannel",
5      "mobiletargeting:UpdateApnsSandboxChannel",
6      "mobiletargeting:UpdateGcmChannel",
7      "mobiletargeting:DeleteApnsChannel",
8      "mobiletargeting:DeleteApnsSandboxChannel",
9      "mobiletargeting:DeleteGcmChannel"
10   ],
11   "Resource": [
12     "arn:aws:mobiletargeting:*:*:apps/*/channels/*"
13   ]
14 }
```

These permissions allow Mobile Hub to manage the channels that Amazon Pinpoint uses to deliver messages to the push notification services for iOS and Android. Mobile Hub creates or updates a channel when you provide your credentials for Apple Push Notification service, Firebase Cloud Messaging, or Google Cloud Messaging. You provide your credentials by using the Mobile Hub console or Amazon Pinpoint console.

IAM Role for Importing Segments

With Amazon Pinpoint, you define a user segment by importing endpoint definitions from an Amazon S3 bucket in your AWS account. Before you import, you must delegate the required permissions to Amazon Pinpoint. Create an AWS Identity and Access Management (IAM) role and attach the following policies to the role:

- The `AmazonS3ReadOnlyAccess` AWS managed policy. This policy is created and managed by AWS, and it grants read-only access to your Amazon S3 bucket.

- A *trust policy* that allows Amazon Pinpoint to assume the role.

For more information about IAM roles, see IAM Roles in the *IAM User Guide*.

After you create the role, you can use Amazon Pinpoint to import segments. For an example of how to import a segment by using the AWS SDK for Java, see Importing Segments. For information about creating the Amazon S3 bucket, creating endpoint files, and importing a segment by using the console, see Importing Segments in the *Amazon Pinpoint User Guide*.

Trust Policy

To allow Amazon Pinpoint to assume the IAM role and perform the actions allowed by the `AmazonS3ReadOnlyAccess` policy, attach the following trust policy to the role:

```
1  {
2    "Version": "2012-10-17",
3    "Statement": [
4      {
5        "Effect": "Allow",
6        "Principal": {
7          "Service": "pinpoint.us-east-1.amazonaws.com"
8        },
9        "Action": "sts:AssumeRole"
10     }
11   ]
12 }
```

Creating the IAM Role (AWS CLI)

Complete the following steps to create the IAM role by using the AWS Command Line Interface (AWS CLI).

If you have not installed the AWS CLI, see Getting Set Up with the AWS Command Line Interface in the *AWS Command Line Interface User Guide*.

To create the IAM role by using the AWS CLI

1. Create a JSON file that contains the trust policy for your role, and save the file locally. You can copy the trust policy provided in this topic.

2. Use the http://docs.aws.amazon.com/cli/latest/reference/iam/create-role.html command to create the role and attach the trust policy:

```
1  aws iam create-role --role-name PinpointSegmentImport --assume-role-policy-document file://
     PinpointImportTrustPolicy.json
```

Following the `file://` prefix, specify the path to the JSON file that contains the trust policy.

When you run this command, the AWS CLI prints the following output in your terminal:

```
 1 {
 2     "Role": {
 3         "AssumeRolePolicyDocument": {
 4             "Version": "2012-10-17",
 5             "Statement": [
 6                 {
 7                     "Action": "sts:AssumeRole",
 8                     "Effect": "Allow",
 9                     "Principal": {
10                         "Service": "pinpoint.us-east-1.amazonaws.com"
11                     }
12                 }
13             ]
14         },
15         "RoleId": "AIDACKCEVSQ6C2EXAMPLE",
16         "CreateDate": "2016-12-20T00:44:37.406Z",
17         "RoleName": "PinpointSegmentImport",
18         "Path": "/",
19         "Arn": "arn:aws:iam::111122223333:role/PinpointSegmentImport"
20     }
21 }
```

3. Use the http://docs.aws.amazon.com/cli/latest/reference/iam/attach-role-policy.html command to attach the AmazonS3ReadOnlyAccess AWS managed policy to the role:

```
 1 aws iam attach-role-policy --policy-arn arn:aws:iam::aws:policy/AmazonS3ReadOnlyAccess --
     role-name PinpointSegmentImport
```

IAM Role for Streaming Events to Kinesis

Amazon Pinpoint can automatically send app usage data, or *event data*, from your app to a Kinesis stream or Amazon Kinesis Data Firehose delivery stream in your AWS account. Before Amazon Pinpoint can begin streaming the event data, you must delegate the required permissions to Amazon Pinpoint.

If you use the console to set up event streaming, Amazon Pinpoint automatically creates an AWS Identity and Access Management (IAM) role with the required permissions. For more information, see Streaming Amazon Pinpoint Events to Amazon Kinesis in the *Amazon Pinpoint User Guide*.

If you want to create the role manually, attach the following policies to the role:

- A permissions policy that allows Amazon Pinpoint to send records to your stream.
- A trust policy that allows Amazon Pinpoint to assume the role.

For more information about IAM roles, see IAM Roles in the *IAM User Guide*.

After you create the role, you can configure Amazon Pinpoint to automatically send events to your stream. For more information, see Streaming Amazon Pinpoint Events to Kinesis.

Permissions Policies

To allow Amazon Pinpoint to send event data to your stream, attach one of the following policies to the role.

Amazon Kinesis Data Streams

The following policy allows Amazon Pinpoint to send event data to a Kinesis stream.

```
1  {
2      "Version": "2012-10-17",
3      "Statement": {
4          "Action": [
5              "kinesis:PutRecords",
6              "kinesis:DescribeStream"
7          ],
8          "Effect": "Allow",
9          "Resource": [
10              "arn:aws:kinesis:region:account-id:stream/stream-name"
11          ]
12      }
13  }
```

Amazon Kinesis Data Firehose

The following policy allows Amazon Pinpoint to send event data to a Kinesis Data Firehose delivery stream.

```
1  {
2      "Version": "2012-10-17",
3      "Statement": {
4          "Effect": "Allow",
5          "Action": [
6              "firehose:PutRecordBatch",
7              "firehose:DescribeDeliveryStream"
8          ],
```

```
 9        "Resource": [
10            "arn:aws:firehose:region:account-id:deliverystream/delivery-stream-name"
11        ]
12    }
13 }
```

Trust Policy

To allow Amazon Pinpoint to assume the IAM role and perform the actions allowed by the permissions policy, attach the following trust policy to the role:

```
 1 {
 2   "Version": "2012-10-17",
 3   "Statement": [
 4     {
 5       "Effect": "Allow",
 6       "Principal": {
 7         "Service": "pinpoint.amazonaws.com"
 8       },
 9       "Action": "sts:AssumeRole"
10     }
11   ]
12 }
```

Creating the IAM Role (AWS CLI)

Complete the following steps to create the IAM role by using the AWS Command Line Interface (AWS CLI).

If you have not installed the AWS CLI, see Getting Set Up with the AWS Command Line Interface in the *AWS Command Line Interface User Guide.*

To create the role by using the IAM console, see Setting up Event Streaming in the *Amazon Pinpoint User Guide.*

To create the IAM role by using the AWS CLI

1. Create a JSON file that contains the trust policy for your role, and save the file locally. You can copy the trust policy provided in this topic.

2. Use the http://docs.aws.amazon.com/cli/latest/reference/iam/create-role.html command to create the role and attach the trust policy:

```
1 aws iam create-role --role-name PinpointEventStreamRole --assume-role-policy-document file
    ://PinpointEventStreamTrustPolicy.json
```

Following the `file://` prefix, specify the path to the JSON file that contains the trust policy.

When you run this command, the AWS CLI prints the following output in your terminal:

```
1 {
2     "Role": {
3         "AssumeRolePolicyDocument": {
4             "Version": "2012-10-17",
5             "Statement": [
6                 {
7                     "Action": "sts:AssumeRole",
8                     "Effect": "Allow",
```

120

```
9          "Principal": {
10              "Service": "pinpoint.amazonaws.com"
11          }
12      }
13      ]
14  },
15  "RoleId": "AIDACKCEVSQ6C2EXAMPLE",
16  "CreateDate": "2017-02-28T18:02:48.220Z",
17  "RoleName": "PinpointEventStreamRole",
18  "Path": "/",
19  "Arn": "arn:aws:iam::111122223333:role/PinpointEventStreamRole"
20  }
21 }
```

3. Create a JSON file that contains the permissions policy for your role, and save the file locally. You can copy one of the policies provided in the Permissions Policies section.

4. Use the http://docs.aws.amazon.com/cli/latest/reference/iam/put-role-policy.html command to attach the permissions policy to the role:

```
1 aws iam put-role-policy --role-name PinpointEventStreamRole --policy-name
      PinpointEventStreamPermissionsPolicy --policy-document file://
      PinpointEventStreamPermissionsPolicy.json
```

Following the `file://` prefix, specify the path to the JSON file that contains the permissions policy.

Limits in Amazon Pinpoint

The following sections describe limits within Amazon Pinpoint.

- General limits
- Endpoint limits
- Endpoint import limits
- Segment limits
- Campaign limits
- Mobile push limits
- Email limits
- SMS limits
- Requesting a limit increase

General limits

The following limits affect general use of Amazon Pinpoint.

Resource	Default Limit	Eligible for Increase
API request payload size	7 MB per request	No
Apps	100 per account	No

Endpoint limits

The following limits apply to the Endpoints resource in the Amazon Pinpoint API.

Resource	Default Limit	Eligible for Increase
Attributes assigned to the `Attributes, Metrics,` and `UserAttributes` parameters collectively	40 per app	No
Attributes assigned to the `Attributes` parameter	40 per app	No
Attributes assigned to the `Metrics` parameter	40 per app	No
Attributes assigned to the `UserAttributes` parameter	40 per app	No
Attribute name length	50 characters	No
Attribute value length	100 characters	No
`EndpointBatchItem` objects in an `EndpointBatchRequest` payload	100 per payload. The payload size can't exceed 7 MB.	No
Endpoints with the same user ID	10 unique endpoints per user ID	No
Values assigned to `Attributes` parameter attributes	50 per attribute	No
Values assigned to `UserAttributes` parameter attributes	50 per attribute	No

Endpoint import limits

The following limits apply when you import endpoints into Amazon Pinpoint.

Resource	Default Limit	Eligible for Increase
Concurrent import jobs	2 per account	Yes
Import size	1 GB per import job(For example, if each endpoint is 4 KB or less, you can import 250,000 endpoints.)	Yes

Segment limits

The following limits apply to the Segments resource in the Amazon Pinpoint API.

Resource	Default Limit	Eligible for Increase
Maximum number of segments	100 per app	No
Maximum number of dimensions that can be used to create a segment	100 per segment	No

Campaign limits

The following limits apply to the Campaigns resource in the Amazon Pinpoint API.

Resource	Default Limit	Eligible for Increase
Active campaigns	200 per account An *active campaign* is a campaign that hasn't completed or failed. Active campaigns have a status of SCHEDULED, EXECUTING, or PENDING_NEXT_RUN.	Yes
Message sends	100 million per campaign activity	Yes

Mobile push limits

The following limits apply to messages that Amazon Pinpoint delivers through mobile push channels.

Resource	Default Limit	Eligible for Increase
Amazon Device Messaging (ADM) message payload size	6 KB per message	No
Apple Push Notification service (APNs) message payload size	4 KB per message	No
APNs sandbox message payload size	4 KB per message	No

Resource	Default Limit	Eligible for Increase
Baidu Cloud Push message payload size	4 KB per message	No
Firebase Cloud Messaging (FCM) or Google Cloud Messaging (GCM) message payload size	4 KB per message	No

Email limits

The limits in the following sections apply to the Email channel.

Email Sending Limits

Resource	Default Limit	Eligible for Increase
Number of emails that can be sent per 24-hour period (sending quota)	If your account is in the sandbox: 200 emails per 24-hour period. If your account is out of the sandbox, the quota varies based on your specific use case. This quota is based on the number of recipients, as opposed to the number of unique messages sent. A *recipient* is any email address on the To: line.	Yes
Number of emails that can be sent each second (sending rate)	If your account is in the sandbox: 1 email per second. If your account is out of the sandbox, the rate varies based on your specific use case. This rate is based on the number of recipients, as opposed to the number of unique messages sent. A *recipient* is any email address on the To: line.	Yes

Email Message Limits

Resource	Default Limit	Eligible for Increase
Maximum message size (including attachments)	10 MB per message.	No

Resource	Default Limit	Eligible for Increase
Number of verified identities	10,000 identities. *Identities* refers to email addresses or domains, or any combination of the two. Every email you send using Amazon Pinpoint must be sent from a verified identity.	No

Email Sender and Recipient Limits

Resource	Default Limit	Eligible for Increase
Sender address	All sending addresses or domains must be verified.	No
Recipient address	If your account is still in the sandbox, all recipient email addresses or domains must be verified. If your account is out of the sandbox, you can send to any valid address.	Yes
Number of recipients per message	50 recipients per message.	No
Number of identities that you can verify	10,000 identities per AWS Region. *Identities* refers to email addresses or domains, or any combination of the two. Every email you send using Amazon Pinpoint must be sent from a verified identity.	No

SMS limits

The following limits apply to the SMS channel.

Resource	Default Limit	Eligible for Increase
Account spend threshold	USD$1.00 per account.	Yes
Number of SMS messages that can be sent each second (*sending rate*)	20 messages per second.	No
Number of Amazon SNS topics for two-way SMS	100,000 per account.	Yes

Requesting a limit increase

If the value in the **Eligible for Increase** column in any of the tables above is **Yes**, you can request a change to that limit.

To request a limit increase

1. Sign in to the AWS Management Console at https://console.aws.amazon.com/.

2. Create a new Support case at htttps://console.aws.amazon.com/support/home#/case/create.

3. On the **Create Case** page, make the following selections:

   - For **Regarding**, choose **Service Limit Increase**.

   - For **Limit Type**, choose one of the following options:

     - Choose **Amazon Pinpoint** for limit increases related to Amazon Pinpoint campaigns and imports.

     - Choose **Amazon Pinpoint Email** for limit increases related to the email channel.

     - Choose **Amazon Pinpoint SMS** for limit increases related to the SMS channel.

4. For **Use Case Description**, explain why you are requesting the limit increase.

5. For **Support Language**, choose the language you prefer to use when communicating with the AWS Support team.

6. For **Contact Method**, choose your preferred method of communicating with the AWS Support team.

7. Choose **Submit**.

Creating Custom Channels with AWS Lambda

This is prerelease documentation for a feature in public beta release. It is subject to change.

Amazon Pinpoint supports messaging channels for mobile push, email, and SMS. However, some messaging use cases might require unsupported channels. For example, you might want to send a message to an instant messaging service, such as Facebook Messenger, or you might want to display a notification within your web application. In such cases, you can use AWS Lambda to create a custom channel that performs the message delivery outside of Amazon Pinpoint.

AWS Lambda is a compute service that you can use to run code without provisioning or managing servers. You package your code and upload it to Lambda as *Lambda functions*. Lambda runs a function when the function is invoked, which might be done manually by you or automatically in response to events.

For more information, see Lambda Functions in the *AWS Lambda Developer Guide*.

To create a custom channel, you define a Lambda function that handles the message delivery for an Amazon Pinpoint campaign. Then, you assign the function to a campaign by defining the campaign's http://docs.aws.amazon.com/pinpoint/latest/apireference/rest-api-campaign.html#rest-api-campaign-attributes-campaignhook-table settings. These settings include the Lambda function name and the `CampaignHook` mode. By setting the mode to `DELIVERY`, you specify that the Lambda function handles the message delivery instead of Amazon Pinpoint.

A Lambda function that you assign to a campaign is referred to as an Amazon Pinpoint *extension*.

With the `CampaignHook` settings defined, Amazon Pinpoint automatically invokes the Lambda function when it runs the campaign, without sending the campaign's message to a standard channel. Instead, Amazon Pinpoint sends *event data* about the message delivery to the function, and it allows the function to handle the delivery. The event data includes the message body and the list of endpoints to which the message should be delivered.

After Amazon Pinpoint successfully invokes the function, it generates a successful send event for the campaign.

Note
You can also use the `CampaignHook` settings to assign a Lambda function that modifies and returns a campaign's segment before Amazon Pinpoint delivers the campaign's message. For more information, see Customizing Segments with AWS Lambda.

To create a custom channel with AWS Lambda, first create a function that accepts the event data sent by Amazon Pinpoint and handles the message delivery. Then, authorize Amazon Pinpoint to invoke the function by assigning a Lambda function policy. Finally, assign the function to one or more campaigns by defining `CampaignHook` settings.

Event Data

When Amazon Pinpoint invokes your Lambda function, it provides the following payload as the event data:

```
1  {
2    "MessageConfiguration": {Message configuration}
3    "ApplicationId": ApplicationId,
4    "CampaignId": CampaignId,
5    "TreatmentId": TreatmentId,
6    "ActivityId": ActivityId,
7    "ScheduledTime": Scheduled Time,
8    "Endpoints": {
9      EndpointId: {Endpoint definition}
10     . . .
```

```
11    }
12  }
```

The event data provides the following attributes:

- **MessageConfiguration** – Has the same structure as the http://docs.aws.amazon.com/pinpoint/latest/apireference/rest-api-messages.html#rest-api-messages-attributes-directmessageconfiguration-table in the **Messages** resource in the Amazon Pinpoint API.

- **ApplicationId** – The ID of the Amazon Pinpoint project to which the campaign belongs.

- **CampaignId** – The ID of the Amazon Pinpoint project for which the function is invoked.

- **TreatmentId** – The ID of a campaign variation used for A/B testing.

- **ActivityId** – The ID of the activity being performed by the campaign.

- **ScheduledTime** – The schedule time at which the campaign's messages are delivered in ISO 8601 format.

- **Endpoints** – A map that associates endpoint IDs with endpoint definitions. Each event data payload contains up to 50 endpoints. If the campaign segment contains more than 50 endpoints, Amazon Pinpoint invokes the function repeatedly, with up to 50 endpoints at a time, until all endpoints have been processed.

Creating a Lambda Function

To create a Lambda function, refer to Building Lambda Functions in the *AWS Lambda Developer Guide*.

Example Lambda Function

The following example Lambda function receives event data when Amazon Pinpoint runs a campaign, and it sends the campaign's message to Facebook Messenger:

```
1  "use strict";
2
3  var https = require("https");
4  var q = require("q");
5
6  var VERIFY_TOKEN = "my_token";
7  var PAGE_ACCESS_TOKEN = "EAF...DZD";
8  /* this constant can be put in a constants file and shared between this function and your
       Facebook Messenger webhook code */
9  var FACEBOOK_MESSENGER_PSID_ATTRIBUTE_KEY = "facebookMessengerPsid";
10
11 exports.handler = function(event, context, callback) {
12
13     var deliverViaMessengerPromises = [];
14
15     if (event.Message && event.Endpoints) {
16         for (var endpoint in event.Endpoints) {
17             if (isFbookMessengerActive(event.Endpoints[endpoint])) {
18                 deliverViaMessengerPromises.push(deliverViaMessenger(event.Message, event.
                     Endpoints[endpoint].User));
19             }
20         }
21     }
22
23     /* default OK response */
```

```
24      var response = {
25          body: "ok",
26          statusCode: 200
27      };
28
29      if (deliverViaMessengerPromises.length > 0) {
30          q.all(deliverViaMessengerPromises).done(function() {
31              callback(null, response);
32          });
33      } else {
34          callback(null, response);
35      }
36
37  }
38
39  /**
40  Example Pinpoint Endpoint User object where we've added custom attribute facebookMessengerPsid
        to store the PSID needed by Facebook's API
41  {
42      "UserId": "7a9870b7-493c-4521-b0ca-08bbbc36e595",
43      "UserAttributes": {
44          "facebookMessengerPsid": [ "1667566386619741" ]
45      }
46  }
47  **/
48  function isFbookMessengerActive(endpoint) {
49      return endpoint.User && endpoint.User.UserAttributes && endpoint.User.UserAttributes[
            FACEBOOK_MESSENGER_PSID_ATTRIBUTE_KEY];
50  }
51
52  /**
53  Sample message object from Pinpoint. This sample was an SMS so it has "smsmessage" attribute but
        this will vary for each messaging channel
54  {
55      "smsmessage": {
56          "body": "This message should be intercepted by a campaign hook."
57      }
58  }
59  **/
60  function deliverViaMessenger(message, user) {
61      var deferred = q.defer();
62
63      var messageText = message["smsmessage"]["body"];
64      var pinpointUserId = user.UserId;
65      var facebookPsid = user.UserAttributes[FACEBOOK_MESSENGER_PSID_ATTRIBUTE_KEY][0];
66      console.log("Sending message for user %s and page %s with message:", pinpointUserId,
            facebookPsid, messageText);
67
68      var messageData = {
69          recipient: {
70              id: facebookPsid
71          },
72          message: {
73              text: messageText
```

```
74          }
75      };
76
77      var body = JSON.stringify(messageData);
78      var path = "/v2.6/me/messages?access_token=" + PAGE_ACCESS_TOKEN;
79      var options = {
80          host: "graph.facebook.com",
81          path: path,
82          method: "POST",
83          headers: {
84              "Content-Type": "application/json"
85          }
86      };
87
88      var req = https.request(options, httpsCallback);
89
90      req.on("error", function(e) {
91          console.log("Error posting to Facebook Messenger: " + e);
92          deferred.reject(e);
93      });
94
95      req.write(body);
96      req.end();
97
98      return deferred.promise;
99
100     function httpsCallback(response) {
101         var str = "";
102         response.on("data", function(chunk) {
103             str += chunk;
104         });
105         response.on("end", function() {
106             console.log(str);
107             deferred.resolve(response);
108         });
109     }
110 }
```

Assigning a Lambda Function Policy

Before you can use your Lambda function to process your endpoints, you must authorize Amazon Pinpoint to invoke your Lambda function. To grant invocation permission, assign a *Lambda function policy* to the function. A Lambda function policy is a resource-based permissions policy that designates which entities can use your function and what actions those entities can take.

For more information, see Using Resource-Based Policies for AWS Lambda (Lambda Function Policies) in the *AWS Lambda Developer Guide*.

Example Function Policy

The following policy grants permission to the Amazon Pinpoint service principal to use the `lambda:InvokeFunction` action:

```
1  {
2    "Sid": "sid",
3    "Effect": "Allow",
4    "Principal": {
5      "Service": "pinpoint.us-east-1.amazonaws.com"
6    },
7    "Action": "lambda:InvokeFunction",
8    "Resource": "{arn:aws:lambda:us-east-1:account-id:function:function-name}",
9    "Condition": {
10     "ArnLike": {
11       "AWS:SourceArn": "arn:aws:mobiletargeting:us-east-1:account-id:/apps/application-id/
               campaigns/campaign-id"
12     }
13   }
14 }
```

Your function policy requires a `Condition` block that includes an `AWS:SourceArn` key. This code states which Amazon Pinpoint campaign is allowed to invoke the function. In this example, the policy grants permission to only a single campaign ID. To write a more generic policy, use multi-character match wildcards (*). For example, you can use the following `Condition` block to allow any Amazon Pinpoint campaign in your AWS account to invoke the function:

```
1  "Condition": {
2    "ArnLike": {
3      "AWS:SourceArn": "arn:aws:mobiletargeting:us-east-1:account-id:/apps/*/campaigns/*"
4    }
5  }
```

Granting Amazon Pinpoint Invocation Permission

You can use the AWS Command Line Interface (AWS CLI) to add permissions to the Lambda function policy assigned to your Lambda function. To allow Amazon Pinpoint to invoke a function, use the Lambda http://docs.aws.amazon.com/cli/latest/reference/lambda/add-permission.html command, as shown by the following example:

```
1  $ aws lambda add-permission \
2  > --function-name function-name \
3  > --statement-id sid \
4  > --action lambda:InvokeFunction \
5  > --principal pinpoint.us-east-1.amazonaws.com \
6  > --source-arn arn:aws:mobiletargeting:us-east-1:account-id:/apps/application-id/campaigns/
       campaign-id
```

If you want to provide a campaign ID for the `--source-arn` parameter, you can look up your campaign IDs by using the Amazon Pinpoint http://docs.aws.amazon.com/cli/latest/reference/pinpoint/get-campaigns.html command with the AWS CLI. This command requires an `--application-id` parameter. To look up your application IDs, sign in to the Amazon Pinpoint console at https://console.aws.amazon.com/pinpoint/, and go to the **Projects** page. The console shows an **ID** for each project, which is the project's application ID.

When you run the Lambda `add-permission` command, AWS Lambda returns the following output:

```
1  {
2    "Statement": "{\"Sid\":\"sid\",
3      \"Effect\":\"Allow\",
4      \"Principal\":{\"Service\":\"pinpoint.us-east-1.amazonaws.com\"},
5      \"Action\":\"lambda:InvokeFunction\",
```

```
 6     \"Resource\":\"arn:aws:lambda:us-east-1:111122223333:function:function-name\",
 7     \"Condition\":
 8       {\"ArnLike\":
 9         {\"AWS:SourceArn\":
10          \"arn:aws:mobiletargeting:us-east-1:111122223333:/apps/application-id/campaigns/
              campaign-id\"}}}"
11 }
```

The `Statement` value is a JSON string version of the statement added to the Lambda function policy.

Assigning a Lambda Function to a Campaign

You can assign a Lambda function to an individual Amazon Pinpoint campaign. Or, you can set the Lambda function as the default used by all campaigns for a project, except for those campaigns to which you assign a function individually.

To assign a Lambda function to an individual campaign, use the Amazon Pinpoint API to create or update a http://docs.aws.amazon.com/pinpoint/latest/apireference/rest-api-campaigns.html object, and define its `CampaignHook` attribute. To set a Lambda function as the default for all campaigns in a project, create or update the http://docs.aws.amazon.com/pinpoint/latest/apireference/rest-api-settings.html resource for that project, and define its `CampaignHook` object.

In both cases, set the following `CampaignHook` attributes:

- `LambdaFunctionName` – The name or ARN of the Lambda function that Amazon Pinpoint invokes to send messages for the campaign.

- `Mode` – Set to `DELIVERY`. With this mode, Amazon Pinpoint uses the function to deliver the messages for a campaign, and it doesn't attempt to send the messages through the standard channels.

Document History for Amazon Pinpoint

The following table describes the documentation for this release of Amazon Pinpoint.

- **Latest documentation update:** February 6, 2018

Change	Description	Date
AWS CloudTrail logging	Added information about logging Amazon Pinpoint API calls with CloudTrail.	February 6, 2018
Updated service limits	Updated Limits in Amazon Pinpoint with additional information about email limits.	January 19, 2018
Public beta for Amazon Pinpoint extensions	Use AWS Lambda functions to customize segments or create custom messaging channels.	November 28, 2017
External ID removed from IAM trust policies	The external ID key is removed from the example trust policy and example Java code for importing segments.	October 26, 2017
Push notification payload limits	The limits include payload sizes for mobile push messages.	October 25, 2017
Updated service limits	Added SMS and email channel information to Limits in Amazon Pinpoint.	October 9, 2017
ADM and Baidu mobile push	Update your app code to handle push notifications from the Baidu and ADM mobile push channels.	September 27, 2017
User IDs and authentication events with Amazon Cognito user pools.	If you use Amazon Cognito user pools to manage user sign-in in your mobile apps, Amazon Cognito assigns user IDs to endpoints, and it reports authentication events to Amazon Pinpoint.	September 26, 2017
User IDs	Assign user IDs to endpoints to monitor app usage from individual users. Examples are provided for the Mobile SDK for iOS, Mobile SDK for Android, and SDK for Java.	August 31, 2017
Authentication events	Report authentication events to learn how frequently users authenticate with your app. Examples are provided for the Mobile SDK for iOS and Mobile SDK for Android.	August 31, 2017
Updated sample events	The example events include events that Amazon Pinpoint streams for email and SMS activity.	June 08, 2017

Change	Description	Date
Android session management	Manage sessions in Android apps by using a class provided by the AWS Mobile Hub sample app.	April 20, 2017
Updated monetization event samples	The sample code is updated for reporting monetization events with the Mobile SDK for iOS and Mobile SDK for Android.	March 31, 2017
Event streams	You can configure Amazon Pinpoint to send your app and campaign events to an Kinesis stream.	March 24, 2017
Permissions	See Permissions for information about granting access to Amazon Pinpoint for AWS users in your account and users of your mobile app.	January 12, 2017
Amazon Pinpoint general availability	This release introduces Amazon Pinpoint.	December 1, 2016

www.ingramcontent.com/pod-product-compliance
Lightning Source LLC
LaVergne TN
LVHW082039050326
832904LV00005B/243

* 9 7 8 9 8 8 8 4 0 8 6 0 3 *